The Pilgrim Season

Finding Your Real Self in Retirement

Roger O. Douglas

FORWARD MOVEMENT
CINCINNATI, OHIO

The Pilgrim Season

FORWARD MOVEMENT
300 West Fourth Street
Cincinnati, Ohio 45202-2666

800-543-1813
www. forwardmovement.org

Table of Contents

Preface

For all that has been, thanks.
For all that shall be, yes.

—Dag Hammarskjöld[1]

In the sense that it is commonly used, the word retirement is a misnomer. There must be another word to define a period when one no longer keeps regular hours doing the work one has been doing day after day for a number of years. Rather than a word that suggests going to bed and covering your head and moving out of the mainstream of life, there should be an upbeat word that suggests a new and exciting experience, an opportunity to explore new ideas and interests, a time to meet new challenges.

After all, there have been many other major transitions in most lives. For example, consider the time a person 1) leaves his/her mother's loving care and enters kindergarten, 2) finishes high school and/or college, 3) lands a full-time job—or perhaps loses one, 4) gets married, or perhaps, divorced. We all make transitions during our lifetimes, and somehow we survive and most often move on to happier days.

Fifty years ago it was more the norm to work until we were physically or mentally worn out or until we died on the job. Now, the picture has radically changed and most of us are granted another opportunity for a transition. We are retiring earlier, living longer, and are active for many years after we discontinue our "official" working life.

Carl Jung[2], as far back as the 1930s, recognized that this stage of life is radically different from the earlier stage. Although he never spoke of retirement as a transition point, he did underline that human beings were quite unprepared for coping with the afternoon of life as opposed to what he called the morning of life. Little is known about this period in the life cycle. Very little has been written about it, and as Jung pointed out, there are no schools to prepare us. Almost 12.4% of our population is already in the over-65 category, and more and more Baby Boomers are reaching that milestone. It seems appropriate at this time to begin a dialogue about this often misunderstood phase of life.

Tried and true formulas for making a successful move from working life to retirement are virtually nonexistent. Rules change, the game shifts, we enter into a new stage of life, and we often wonder what is happening. Suddenly, we are asked to invest ourselves in a new existence, hoping that something will emerge to give us meaning and replace the emptiness that inevitability comes when we leave the 9-to-5 lifestyle.

As an Episcopal priest for 44 years, I gleaned many bits of wisdom from a vast range of parishioners and colleagues who had faced or were facing a transition from the vibrant, working stage of life to a stage sometimes categorized as "over the hill." Then as we entered a new millennium, I too was faced with that transition. In the process I lost some important parts of me. I lost a piece of my identity. A short while earlier I had been The Reverend Dr. Roger O. Douglas, rector. Suddenly I became just plain Roger Douglas. Sure, "The Reverend" is still there, but I no longer have the community that looked to me as one of its leaders. Now my community, as with most other retirees, is my wife, my family, and my friends.

The time since my own retirement has given me an opportunity to take a deep breath and to watch more closely my friends and colleagues who have gone through or are going through this process. I have consciously interviewed men and women who have experienced retirement and asked them to reveal the pros and cons of their lives today.

The purpose of this book, then, is to be thought of as a conversation with the reader, a vehicle to help those about to retire or those already retired explore the inner journey one takes in retirement. Throughout this transition the word pilgrimage comes to mind, because that word is a powerful metaphor for a journey one takes to find meaning.

As we begin our pilgrimage, all that can be projected is there are some common experiences and similar feelings that all of us seem to go through. Having made that assertion, we also have to admit that each person's retirement is unique. The situation that caused this change in our life's journey, the age it took place, and the financial and health circumstances are as varied as the people who experience this transition. To meet the challenge of this diversity, I have sought answers from many retired friends and acquaintances and incorporated their comments throughout this book. Their names, of course, have been changed in order to preserve privacy, but their comments are real. So now, as we take this journey together, perhaps we will discover some secrets of this stage of life that will bring fulfillment to our lives and our souls.

CHAPTER ONE

The Great Adventure

*At every moment you choose yourself. But do
you really choose yourself? Body and soul con-
tain a thousand possibilities out of which you
can build many I's. But only in one of them is
there a congruence of the elect and the elected.*

—Dag Hammarskjöld[1]

Several months ago, in a standard line between
adults and kids, I asked a grandchild, "What do you
want to be when you grow up?" He answered confidently that he wanted to be a firefighter—no doubt a
result of a recent preschool visit to a local fire station.
I can still recall some of my own responses to that
question. They ranged from wanting to be a police-
man to wishing to run a grocery store. Usually, both
adults and children have no expectations that the
response to the question will have any relevance to
one's future life.

"What do you want to be?" Innocuous as the
question sounds, it takes on meaning when asked of
one who is about to retire.

"What do you want to be in retirement?" is the

key to entering this next stage of our lives. Immediate family, cultural factors, and educational opportunities are important ingredients in shaping our futures when we are young, but when we retire they begin to lose their significance. Retirement wipes the slate clean, or, at the very least, alters our perceptions of these factors.

All the former influences, which when young seemed of consequence, no longer have the same meaning. Suddenly we are faced with a golden opportunity. We can answer anew the question: "What do you want to be when you grow up?" Only this time we are much freer to choose our own answer. The possibility of seeing our lives in a new and exciting way stands before us. It is as if we are given a second chance to rewrite the scenarios of our lives.

This realization dawns when we begin to comprehend that we no longer will have the constraints of earning a living. We are no longer tied down to a place of work. Like a bolt from the blue, we are faced with choices that always seemed to have been made by factors beyond our control.

This sense of freedom, of being able to answer the question, "What do I want to be?" puts us at very disquieting crossroads. We can plunge into a chronically anxious state, asking, "Where are all the familiar boundaries? Who gives us the license to practice?" Those comfortable constraints that shaped our everyday lives are now withdrawn. The predictable no longer exists, and for many, this is bad news.

In the corporate world there are those who recognize the comfort of predictability. For example, years ago, Holiday Inns of America® seemed to understand this anxiety better than most of us. They built a business on the predictable. There are few if any surprises. You can count on the same dependable, familiar surroundings. Those who created the concept seemed to believe, as many of us do, that in sameness there is safety. We resist change, keeping the *status quo* seems to be a safe alternative in a fast changing world. It can be boring for some, but it's preferable to the anxiety that comes with having to make choices or face the unexpected.

Whether we like it or not, retirement puts us at such crossroads. We can anxiously try not to make new choices, to hold on to as much of our old lives as possible. Or we can take the risk of turning the corner, moving down a new road, and reinventing ourselves.

In Robertson Davies' novel, *The Manticore*,[2] one of the characters exclaims: "Between a certain age, everybody has to turn a corner in his life or smash into a brick wall."

This is to say there are moments for all of us when, unless we turn that corner, we are headed for a brick wall. I think we come to that point at retirement. If we do not venture out and take the risk of leaving the past, we are courting the possibility of having a boring or monotonous existence. Retirement provides the opportunity to ask the question again, "What am I going to be?" and then to move into the new, the untried, the unexpected.

The great obstacle to doing this is that we have been taught from a very young age to accept the wisdom of the so-called authority figures. We've been told what we can expect when we reach a certain age, and we rarely go beyond the predictable when thinking about retirement life. Conventional wisdom from the experts tells us that you can't teach an old dog new tricks. When we buy into that wisdom we begin to believe that change is not a real possibility. Beware: that is the beginning of "hitting the brick wall."

Harry Chapin,[3] a folk singer, tried to show us what happens when we begin to rely on the wisdom of authority figures. One of his songs is about a young boy who goes to school and begins to use crayons. He draws flowers and leaves in a great profusion of colors until a teacher comes along and begins to "straighten him out," telling him that flowers are red and leaves are green and that's the way they should be colored. The little boy protests, saying he sees many colors in the rainbow and the sun and wants to use them all. The teacher puts him in the corner until finally he succumbs to her wishes.

Time passes and the boy moves to another town and another school, where the smiling teacher says there are many colors in flowers and painting should be fun. Still, the little boy colors all the flowers red and the leaves green. When asked why, he replies, "There's no need to color flowers any other way than the way they have always been seen." It's a sad song, a tragedy in many ways, but it reminds us of how all of us have been taught to accept, without questioning, the way authority figures see the world.

In a way, Chapin's song is a parable about retirement. Do we stop growing when we retire? Do we buy into what people have told us about this stage of life? Do we follow the old tried and true ways? Do we hit a brick wall when we reach a certain age? Throughout these pages the mindset that says you can't change will be challenged. Retirement is as much about unlearning as it is about learning. Retirement is not about stopping growth, not about solving problems. Retirement is about a transition to another stage of life where we can begin to answer anew the question: "What do I want to be?"

Among those interviewed for this book was John, a former owner and CEO of a chain of stores. I met him at his club. He drove up in his Bentley, which made the rest of us in our Fords and Toyotas feel that we ought to look for a new model.

After a leisurely lunch, I began the interview with John. My first question was what convinced him to retire at the age of 53.

"The time was right. Three large companies were interested in buying my business and economic conditions were changing. I was sole proprietor, and I didn't want to go public, because I had seen what that had done to other owners of businesses. The other thing is I had lost control of the business. It seemed to have gotten too large. Before, when we opened a new store, I would go there and help get it started, or go to Brazil or some other place to buy materials. Now it was all done by others; it was no longer a hands-on operation for me.

"I recall walking into one of my stores in another city and a young twenty-something manager walked up to me and said, 'Would you please mind getting out from behind the counter?' I realized that I was out of touch. It was time to retire."

"What happened after you retired?" I asked. "Well, I really didn't believe I had retired. I now could do anything I wanted and live anywhere I wanted, but I hadn't made any plans for retirement. I'd get up at 6 in the morning, get dressed, but there wasn't any work to go to. I'd call some of my contemporaries and say: 'Let's go play some cards or tennis.' They would all laugh and remind me that they were still working. I realized I was becoming boring, so I decided to do some consulting. Initially this turned out to be less than satisfactory. I quickly found out that when people hire you to consult, they make the decisions and you don't. This was particularly frustrating for someone who prided himself on managing things."

He went on to explain that he thinks people who

retire have to validate themselves: "I've worked all my life and have to feel involved. How much bridge can you play? A golf score of 80 is enough for some, but not for me. Maybe you don't have to make money, but you do have to feel that you're worth something. I found validation in two ways. One, in consulting. I do that only when I find something I like. And the other thing is that I became active in my church. I went to church before I retired, but now I'm fully involved in everything from the school to the leadership. I serve at the altar, and I'm on the Bishop's committee.

"One other thing," he said, "if you have a major surgery, as I did a few years ago, it causes you to rethink your religion."

In spite of his upbeat attitude, John confessed that he does have some concerns. "I still love to spend money, but now I have to question whether I can afford things. And I'm very much aware of my health. I guess I'm also more aware of the condition of my soul. Getting ready to die is a frightening thing. When you've been used to going first-class, you don't want anything but the best. I'm not sure what that means in terms of heaven," he laughed, "but I know that I want to be number one."

While John's tale of retirement might be that of a minority of retirees, it is comforting to know that it is possible to find enjoyment and fulfillment in retirement. Some people retire in their 60s and they die but are not buried until in their 80s. Others live until they stop breathing. Retirement is not about loss or diminishment. Retirement is about choosing to turn the corner, letting go of the way things used to be, and starting the pilgrimage to find your real self.

CHAPTER TWO

Choosing the Right Time

*The alternatives are simple, terrifyingly simple
and clear. To compromise is to decide; to hide
the matter is to decide. There is no escape. You
must say yes or no. There are a thousand ways
of saying no. One way of saying yes, and no way
of saying anything else.*

—Author Unknown

One question often raised by those approaching
retirement is: When is the right time to stop working? For some, the question is easily resolved.
Factors outside of our immediate control determine
the answer. We've reached a certain age, or the company (because of economic conditions) hands us
an opportunity to step down with a good financial
package. This has become so popular that a new
phrase has entered our everyday vocabulary, the
golden parachute. For others, the question of when
is answered by health considerations. Medical consultants advise us to begin to take it easy.

The experts suggest that when we have reached
certain financial goals this constitutes the time to

say yes to retirement. The problem is that many of these factors fail to take into account the internal dialogue that takes place as we contemplate the end of a career. Saying yes to retirement is not necessarily about relinquishing our jobs. On an inner level, retirement is a message that we are getting older and therefore much closer to the grave. Some also view retirement as a time when we become defenseless and more helpless in a world that values youthful energy.

It is easy to say, "No, not now," when we see contemporaries who retire and have become bored or tell us they should have worked a little longer to sustain their non-earning years. It is not as easy to say yes and then to boldly set a date for this large transition when the future seems so unclear.

Even when we notice our enthusiasm for the job is waning, or our colleagues seem to be getting younger and younger (or is it that we are getting older?), we find it difficult to say yes to retirement. There are so many unanswered questions, so many paths we might take, and so many adjustments. Framing the confusion is the up-in-the-air quality that many people experience as they approach retirement. Does retirement signal a failure, or is it a reward for a job well done? W.H. Auden,[1] in one of his sonnets, refers to modern people as being "lost upon the mountains of our choice." This certainly is the feeling of many as they contemplate the retirement dilemma.

In many interviews, I found people making the decision only after their jobs began to lose meaning. In retrospect, they wished they had said yes several years earlier. As Harry, one of the interviewees said: "I had done all that a thousand times and wasn't prepared to do it once more 'with feeling.' I just kept thinking: I've been there and done that and I need to refocus my life."

After the initial decision to retire, many interviewed people expressed ambivalence about that decision: "One day I felt confident about the decision; the next day I was set to work another year or two. The risk was not only in making the wrong decision; the risk was not understanding what my decision entailed."

Peter, a middle-management person, said: "As in love and war, timing is everything. In order for my retirement to be more than changing the place where I spend most of my working hours, the timing had to be right. I knew that I would never have enough money to be financially secure against unforeseen disasters. Therefore, I began to look for signals within myself."

Many people who were interviewed reported that they had started the retirement process a good year or more before they realized or before they had officially said anything about their decision. Consciously or unconsciously, they began to develop habits and to make plans that would ease their transition.

Sam, a university professor, said: "In retrospect, I realized I had been preparing myself for several years. For example, I started my garden, and I created two brand new courses. After I announced that I was retiring, several colleagues asked: 'Why do you do that when you only have a few years left? Why not just continue your old lectures?' I never wanted to just continue and slowly fade away. As I moved towards retirement I became more focused. I was only partially aware of this, but the last class I taught was the fulfillment of the key ideas I had held for a long time. To go on after that would be gratuitous."

The more task-oriented people were quite certain when to say yes to retirement. Many of these people set specific goals, such as the completion of some project that could act as a signal to themselves and the world that it was the right time to move on to a new chapter.

In our time there seems to be a trend towards early retirement. This is easier to do when the way we earn our living is not inexplicably bound to our identity. As Jack, an architect, asked: "How do you switch from being 'Jack the architect' for forty-five years, to being just plain 'Jack?'" Later in our interview he shared the way he made the transition: "I found the time was right when I could change the way I measured success. Before I was ready to retire, I measured success by the product and its acceptance by my client. I was ready to retire when I began to use personal satisfaction as my primary measurement. I asked questions, such as, 'Have I learned something in what I'm doing? Have I grown as a person? Have I enjoyed what I'm now doing?' Answers to these questions became more important when I decided to retire."

For Jack, the time was right when he switched his measurements of success. For others, the transition time is not quite as clear. We say yes to retirement with fear and trembling. There are no crystal balls to tell us if our decision is right. There are few indications of what the next ten or twenty years will be like.

Ralph, a C.E.O. of his company, had this to say: "I'm a very systematic person. I had a list of pros and cons. I asked myself these questions: 'Are you willing to change the pace of your life? Can you put aside the demands of work and begin thinking like a person who has the freedom to choose any number of new challenges?'"

A mentor of mine suggested that the time for retirement would be right if: 1) I could leave on the top of the wave. And, 2) I was ready to set my own priorities. "Remember," he told me, "you will be doing things on your own timeline."

We often focus on endings. This compounds the difficulty in deciding when to retire. It is simpler to say "yes, I am ready" when we can concentrate on the future. We are enabled to say yes when we are ready to claim our own existence, when we are ready to take responsibility for our new life. Retirement is a matter of stepping out boldly, even when we are unsure what the future will bring.

Sarah, one of the interviewees, shared a short poem, which she said she kept on her bedroom mirror as she struggled with her approaching retirement:

> *Come to the edge.*
> *No we will fall.*
> *Come to the edge.*
> *No we will fall.*
> *He pushed her.*
> *And she flew.*

—Author unknown

CHAPTER THREE

Finding a New Path

Who am I? This or the other?
Am I one person today and tomorrow another?
Am I both at once a hypocrite before others?
And before myself a contemptible woebegone
        weakling?
Or is something within me still like a beaten
        army,
Fleeing in disorder from victory already
        achieved?
Who am I? They mock me these lonely questions
        of mine.
Whoever I am, thou knowest, O God, I am thine.

—Dietrich Bonhoeffer[1]

Do you remember a time in your life when you discovered you weren't who you thought you were? Discoveries like that often happen as we move from one stage of life to another. They are often associated with loss and cause us to take stock of our lives. For some, the discovery comes in a divorce or other broken relationship. For others, it comes when we begin to realize that the scripts laid out for us are just not adequate. And for still others, it comes when we are fired from a job and wake up to find ourselves unemployed. There are millions of ways that we can be confronted with the discovery of "I'm not who I thought I was." And each time this happens, we stop and agonize over "Who do I really want to be?"

Forces outside of our control often choose our identities for us. The way people look at us, the advertisements we read and sometimes believe, the hints we receive from friends, the reflections we see in the mirror—all contribute to this thing called, "Who am I?" So, how would you describe your own identity? Do you succumb to the categories that society places on those who retire? Would you answer the identity question by saying: "I am elderly. I am a senior citizen. I'm slightly long in the tooth." Or might you use other categories to describe your emerging person? Somehow from within us a message arises that says: "Frogs can become princes and Cinderellas can become queens."

Soon after my retirement, my wife, Peggy, and I visited England. One day I was standing on a crowded bus that was swaying rather vigorously, making it difficult for standing passengers to stay balanced. A middle-aged lady, who was sitting directly across from where I was hanging onto a strap for dear life, caught my eye. She stood up, smiled, and offered me her seat. It was a disturbing moment. I discovered that not everyone saw me as a youthful, solid, athletic figure of a man. There were some, at least in England, who considered me a candidate for being "looked after." Courtesy is one thing, but a discovery like that can be extremely disorienting and sometimes it can even be hurtful. Nevertheless, I took the offered seat.

We avoid examples that inform us that we are older than we would like to be. For many of us, old age equates with senility and moving closer to that stage characterized by uselessness. Our society as a whole seems to express the message that the older you are, the less you are worth.

This was most evident when an elderly neighbor of mine was recently diagnosed with cancer. It was a type treatable by a new drug therapy, but he was informed that people over the age of 60 were not allowed access to the drug because of its scarcity. It was to be released only to those who had a good chance of living 10 to 20 more years. We watched and prayed and cried as this wonderfully wise, gentle, and funny man slowly died for lack of the proper drugs.

During World War I, on the battlefields of Europe a tragic but necessary strategy for emergency medical treatment came into being. It was called "triage." Triage meant sorting the wounded into three categories. Group 1 consisted of those who were only superficially wounded and who would probably recover without much help. Group 2 were those who were more seriously wounded, but who might respond to immediate treatment. And in Group

3 were those who were most severely wounded. Because of the shortage of medical personnel and supplies, only Group 2 received medical aid. In this system of triage, Groups 1 and 3 were refused help. The superficially wounded would probably live, and the severely wounded were abandoned. Group 3 was written off. The thought was why waste precious medical supplies on those who had little chance of recovering?

I think society now utilizes the principle of triage in ministering to people. Only now it's not the severity of the wound so much as the age of the patient. Somehow we have convinced ourselves that a 40-year-old can add more to a society for a longer period of time than a 70-year-old. The 40-year-old is put in Category 2, treatable. The 70-year-old is in Category 3, and therefore kept comfortable.

In many respects this is the direct opposite of the Asian understanding of life, although Asian society also divides life into three categories. These categories are usually referred to as "seasons." In the first season, one is referred to as a student. The student is not held in as high regard as the other categories. In this season of life, one learns, one is tutored, one observes. The second season of life is that of the householder. Here one goes out to manage one's world and endeavors to enter into commerce. The last season in the Asian tradition is the most important. It is called the pilgrim season. In this stage, one leaves those responsibilities of the householder—

making money, raising a family, providing a home—and concentrates on seeking knowledge of oneself. The pilgrim is one who constantly wrestles with the question, "Who am I?" The pilgrim is involved in the most important quest and, therefore, is the one who would be the object of medical attention, if there needed to be a choice.

Shortly after my own retirement I was asked by the leader of a meeting to identify myself. Panic gripped me. I realized, perhaps for the first time, that I had no recognizable title. (I suppose that's one reason some organizations award a retired person the title "emeritus" but that hadn't happened to me.) How to respond? Should I start by telling of my past? Should I simply indicate who I am by saying, "I'm retired and looking for a tennis game." What kind of an identity did I have other than as a retired elderly person with several outside interests? What could I do? Well, I mentioned my name and declared that I was a pilgrim. "A pilgrim?" someone jokingly asked, "What does that mean? Are you old enough to have come over on the Mayflower?"

"No," I replied, "I am a pilgrim on an inner journey. My kind of pilgrim seeks knowledge of oneself and is working toward inner wisdom and more harmony." There was a long silence in the group for I had spoken about an identity, which, at best, was countercultural.

The designation of pilgrim can be a wonderfully free identity. The pilgrim no longer needs to be concerned with producing or accomplishing. The pilgrim focuses on the inner journey of discovery. There is hope that such an inward journey will not lead to pain and confusion, but in the end, will become a homecoming for a person who has been a stranger too long. The pilgrim is set on this journey home, and thus is of great importance to society. There is a sense in which we yearn to see ourselves on the journey. For then we can understand that we do not need to prove or win or produce anything. It's at those moments that I can hug myself and say: "You're a good person, so why don't you relax and enjoy life a little more?"

According to the dictionary, the word *pilgrim* derives from the Latin *pilgrims*, which stands for *foreigner* or *wayfarer*. The older derivation has its roots in the Latin, *per agram*, which translates *through the field*. This suggests that a pilgrim is a person who walks beyond known boundaries. As we transition beyond the boundaries of work and our everyday known world, we start a journey or pilgrimage toward greater meaning.

Identity crisis is a term used by many sociologists. It describes what people go through, as they grow older. Most of us go through several of these identity crises, as we grow older. Retirement is only one of many times when the identity question gets raised. In retirement the question may not be so much, "Who am I?" but rather, "Who am I becoming?" If we are able to view this "crisis" as a pilgrimage rather than a time of loss, the bumps and turns that we experience will somehow be a lot less traumatic. If we view this time as the pilgrim season, our journey will be an interior one and so it doesn't matter whether we go to Bangkok or our backyard, we are still on an important journey.

At every stage of life we are forging an identity, and forging an identity is difficult work. First, we must put aside all that we have been told and risk starting with a blank page. Then we must get in touch with what, in religious terms, is often labeled our "real calling" or why we were put on this earth. And finally, we have to look at all that happens along the way as a part of a sacred journey, a journey in which we find our true selves and discover the paths to which we have been called. Copying someone else can be a barrier, because it can keep us from discovering our unique selves. As this process emerges, we have to be willing to try out some new paths to see if they have heart. If the truth is known, we are always in process and choosing new ways to find meaning. What we need to watch out for is how good a fit there is in the paths we choose today and what challenges we face in the future.

Among the people interviewed for this book was Jeff, a psychologist who had retired about two years earlier. He described those two years: "Sure there were losses after retirement, but I learned to handle losses when I was a kid. I was in bed at age 11 for one year as a result of rheumatic fever. I lost a lot of friends. That taught me about being alone, and how there is a kind of reciprocity in relationships.

"And then later on," he continued, "I learned that you have to face things and still go forward. I stuttered in high school, and as a form of therapy, I tried out for plays. It was a difficult path for a young boy, but through it I learned to confront things, and by facing challenges, you can move ahead."

When asked what he would title a book about his retirement, he replied: "I think if I had to give it a good title, it would be: 'Retirement Life is a Serendipitous Experience.'"

Jeff's implication is that you can make all the plans you want, choose to go down many paths, but life continues, and that's where chance and serendipity come in.

C. S. Lewis wrote: "This world is a great sculpture shop. We are the statues and there is a rumor going around that some of us are some day going to come to life."[2] As pilgrims, we need not see ourselves simply as retirees. On our journey, we can see ourselves coming alive as we face this new stage of our existence.

CHAPTER FOUR:

The Way of the Pilgrim

*The path of development is the fishtailing course
we follow as we let go of what we have been and
then discover a new thing to become—only to
let go of that in time and become something new.
This is the way of transition.*

—William Bridges[1]

After about a year of retirement I was feeling quite comfortable with the transition into the new stage of life. I was busily doing a number of things I had always intended to do, but never was able to find the time nor the energy for. Our social life had improved for it was no longer restricted to Fridays and Saturdays. We also were fortunate in having a grandchild living in the same community. The time spent in babysitting gave us the opportunity to observe this child's development. Life was good. I recall writing a Christmas letter to family and friends indicating our feelings of contentment. I wrote that the two of us go through each day singing, "Sunrise, sunset, swiftly moves the day." This might have been a slight exaggeration, but isn't that what Christmas letters are for?

Then one afternoon, I ran into a friend. She said that from her experience my description of retirement only fit the second stage of the transition and that I had a long way to go before joining the ranks of the fully retired.

American author William Bridges has written extensively about transitions. He often refers to this second stage as the "neutral zone." In this neutral zone we find ourselves looking backwards and forwards, saying goodbyes and hellos at the same time. For some, it's a period of great contentment in which we begin to relax before entering into the final phase of a transition. For others, it can be a period of profound reflection, when we begin to take the first faltering steps towards becoming a new person. Whether we are sitting "at ease in Zion" or busily taking a few faltering steps to reinvent ourselves, there is in the back of our minds that this is a time to try several paths and thus find which direction the future will hold for us.

Bridges credits Arnold van Gennep, a Dutch anthropologist, as originally identifying this neutral zone in the process of transition. It was Gennep who coined the now popular term: *rites of passage*. Van Gennep pointed out that such rites were the way in which people living in traditional societies structured their lives. Van Gennep made this discovery while studying primitive tribes. His findings show that people seem to go through three stages. He identified these as separation, ordeal, and incorporation. This cycle of change demands a break with the past, the enduring of some testing, and finally a return to the ordinary.

In Chapter Three, we talked about assuming the rather archaic title of "pilgrim." Living as if we are pilgrims allows us the time to become aware of the nature of the pilgrimage. There are other words to describe this journey: psychological words, poetic words, and sociological words. Pilgrimage seems to be the most satisfying without carrying a lot of baggage. During the neutral zone stage, we have an opportunity to connect with our souls in an exciting way. As we reflect on the past and anticipate the future we can view parts of our life as being authentic, worthy of future exploration, and other parts as superficial and not suitable for the spending of our time and energy.

In conducting interviews with retirees, I met Margaret, who had retired from a county probation department three years earlier. She seemed to have done a good job of reflecting in the neutral zone before moving ahead. Having retired two years before her husband, she said those two years were her "training for retirement. It was such a big difference in my life. People actually said I was different, more relaxed. I guess I felt as if I was finally free."

Decision time came when she and her husband purchased a home in another area, which meant moving away from their children who lived in the same town. She said that decision represented the realization that their children were finally adults. In describing the situation, she said, "Children have their own lives, and you start thinking, where do you want to end up? I think you see children differently as they get older."

She also feels her children see her in a different light. "I think children think you are always going to be there, but once you retire, they begin to remember what happened with grandparents and they know your years are limited." She said she actually sees more of her children than she did when they lived in the same town.

"I realize that with some of my children I won't be there for them all I wanted to be, she said, "But after a while I was able to say: 'So, O.K. Let's get on with the next phase of our lives. Enjoy what you have left of life.' My husband and I are open. If they [the children] want to be a part of our new life they can. We love it when they are."

Essentially, Margaret's physical departure from her children, starting a new life elsewhere, and finally establishing a new and satisfying relationship with her children is a movement into the next stage of her pilgrimage.

Using the pilgrimage metaphor and combining it with Van Gennep's passages, the retirement journey might be described as departure, arrival, and return, or saying goodbye, saying hello, and finally coming home. T. S. Eliot said it so well in "Little Gidding": "And the end of all our exploring will be to arrive where we started. And know the place for the first time." [2] A pilgrimage is a remembrance that the journey is where our story began and will end. During the pilgrimage we fashion our best selves. Our inward journey is where we can shape our world to be a place of beauty and holiness. Here is where we can intentionally seek God.

The final stage of coming home often is one where everything may look familiar, but one is changed internally because of the pilgrimage. One feels different, one sees differently, one might even act differently, but it is the same old landscape. There is a Zen saying, "After enlightenment, the laundry." In other words after a great change or metamorphosis, we still have to go back to the real world, doing our day-to-day chores. After a journey we still have to take out the garbage and make the beds.

Many writers have used the metaphor of a pilgrimage to describe the inner journey we take as we move through life. Geoffrey Chaucer used the pilgrimage to set his *Canterbury Tales* in a context. Thinking back, we might recall that as each character tells his or her tale, it is in effect describing the way one faces life and the path one chooses. The purpose of Chaucer's work was to describe a journey one takes on our way from home and as we move toward home. The purpose of this circular journey is to show how one transitions from one stage of life to another.

Excerpts from the *Canterbury Tales* are often used

in retirement seminars. Participants are asked to use this as a backdrop for their own stories. Chaucer starts his tale by using the imagery of spring. He uses this metaphor as a waking up to new and exciting events. And so, too, we start out saying retirement can be seen as a waking up to a pilgrimage that is an adventure we are invited to take. A little later in the seminar the participants are encouraged to imagine they too are sitting together at an inn. The host, as in Chaucer's tale, presents a plan to the travelers. Each pilgrim is to tell a tale. Whoever tells the best will be treated to dinner by the rest. Thus, we try to recreate our own pilgrimage to Canterbury.

The members of the seminar are asked to focus on the same question as Chaucer. The question is: Who are you? The participants, similar to Chaucer's characters, do this by answering how they have come to be at the seminar. All participants share their goals for retirement. And in the process of telling the stories of their lives, the participants (like Chaucer's group) pool their knowledge of the journey, merging bits of wisdom, remembering the stories told by others, and revealing much of their inner selves.

Then it is suggested that participants give a title to their own stories. Some of the titles are quite imaginative. Here are samples: "The Leap Towards Freedom," "The Long Snooze," "Fun and Games Forever," "Why Didn't I Do It Sooner," or "I Didn't Deserve the Accolades, but I Also Didn't Deserve the Arthritis."

The leaders of these seminars are alert to what risks the participants are willing to take to attain their goals. What kinds of people have the same hopes and dreams? And finally, what kind of help are they willing to accept in making the journey?

Of course, the major discovery people make in these seminars is that ultimately the goal that we all seek in our journey is not some reality out there. Our common goal is the awakening of a new identity that lies within each participant. Our journey is never to some distant place, but rather it is to perceive the world through a new set of eyes.

The central question is how during retirement do we find significance or renew a sense of vision. The hope is that in the process the retirees will re-define themselves and see life as a journey, or possibly even as a sacred quest to which all of us are invited. The great problem for many who retire is that they simply view what has happened to them as a change and not a real journey. A change is simply a shift in where we are or what we are doing. A journey or a pilgrimage involves us in a process of entering into a search for meaning, and discovering the person that lies within.

It has been observed, as a result of these seminars, that the more one can take on the idea of a pilgrim on a sacred journey, the easier it is to alter one's perspective on life's hardships. What was once a problem becomes a test. What was once a disappointment becomes a challenge. What was viewed as a failure becomes a message to let go and move in another direction.

Almost a half century ago, Professor H. Richard Niebuhr, lecturing at Yale Divinity School, said: "Pilgrims are persons in motion, passing through territories not their own, seeking something we might call completion, or perhaps the word clarity will do as well."

To understand ourselves as pilgrims is the task of those of us who are in the neutral zone. The more we recognize our pilgrimage, the easier it becomes to transition into something new.

CHAPTER FIVE:

Say it Isn't So

In the morning
After taking a cold shower
What a mistake
I look at the mirror
There's a funny guy
Gray hair, white beard, wrinkled skin
What a pity
Poor dirty old man
He is not me, absolutely
I sit down quietly in the lotus position
Meditating, meditating for nothing
Suddenly, a voice comes to me
To stay young
To save the world
Break the mirror.

—Nanao Sakari[1]

A few years ago, I was faced with purchasing a hearing aid. It was either that or learn to read lips. In meetings, counseling people with quiet voices, and in crowded rooms, it had become increasingly difficult to hear all that was being said. Still, I found myself reluctant to be fitted for a device to enhance hearing. Reflecting upon this behavior, I became increasingly aware of associating hearing aids with older people. When finally making a purchase, I only bought a device for one ear. If anyone were to ask, I then could reply: "Oh, I've always had a bad ear." This way I could sidestep being placed in the category of older people.

It has been said that little children live in a world that is 75% fantasy and 25% reality. You can see it in their play. Educators go on to say that by the age of eight, a child's world is reversed and is 75% reality and 25% fantasy. Great changes take place during that time. *Cinderella* and *Winnie the Pooh* are about such transitions. The switch can be from fantasy to reality. But if the transition is from childhood fantasy, which is charming, to adult fantasy, it can become a real problem.

Recently at a party, a stranger approached me and asked what I do for a living. I mumbled something about writing a book. Denial is a very ancient way to handle what is unacceptable. And so we twist and turn in order to avoid embracing certain realities. And some of us even move into adult illusions.

Roger Gould is author of a book entitled, *Transformation: Growth and Change in the Adult Years*.[2] It is about the adult life cycle and the predictable crises we encounter along the way. His basic thesis is that if we can put aside the myths, those erroneous assumptions that enable us to remain in denial, we then might grow into another stage of life.

For example, the assumption we often have in our 20s is that if we keep the rules and do what is expected, somehow life will be smooth sailing. We can maintain that fiction only by strongly denying the slings and arrows that are a part of everyday life. And so it is with retirement. The assumption we often hold onto is that retirement will not mean that a major life change is taking place. We deny the fact that retirement signifies major losses—physical, mental, and often financial. We screen out the negative aspects of retirement and forget that we have to lose some things in order to gain others.

One of the great temptations is to deny that we are at the retirement stage of life. We can maintain that deception by saying we have retired from one job, but have started a new career. It may be possible to switch careers, but this doesn't negate that retirement marks the ending of one stage of life and the beginning of another.

According to Gould, the ability to identify and set aside those myths is the key to growth. The reason we quickly forget the teachings of someone like Gould is that denial is so much easier, and furthermore we know that we can't predict what retirement will be like. If it is truly to be a new stage, then many of the old tried-and-true myths we have depended upon will be upset. And if we are honest, the last thing most of us want to live with is uncertainty, even if our former life was not perfect or was not what we would have chosen. Most of us prefer the security of known misery to the misery of unfamiliar insecurity. "Oh, I'm not retired," we say, "I'm just pursuing other forms of work."

Uncertainty is something we must deal with in retirement. Yes, there is uncertainty *before* we retire, but in the retirement stage of life there is the realization that there are fewer years and fewer opportunities to correct any mistakes we make. One of my interviews revealed some of the uncertainties. Jim, an architect and administrator of construction and design for a major university, had retired a year earlier.

"I worry a lot about our family economics," he said. "I am not comfortable with the balance between income and our style of living. There are new costs involved in being retired, and then there are things you don't spend money on that you did in the past.

"There is a certain uneasiness of not having a job that has escalating income. We're not facing a disaster, but it isn't as orderly as it was when I was working," he said. "Retirement is still a mystery to me."

In spite of the uncertainty, Jim was not in a state of denial. He expressed a sense of enthusiasm and acceptance of his retirement years. "For my wife and me, retirement represents a time for exploration. We are expecting retirement to give us new horizons. We look forward to seeing new and different places and using our roots as a basis for moving forward."

In the past 10 years there have been many studies made on the cost we pay for denial. This has been dramatically shown in the research with terminally ill persons. Maintaining the myth that one is not in the last stage of life often keeps one from creatively accepting death. The more we realistically understand and can talk to those close to us about the terminal situation, the easier it is to use this circumstance as a means of growth.

And so it is with retirement. If we realistically face this stage and come to terms with the fact that we will be different people in different situations, the chances of using retirement as a step into a great adventure are greatly enhanced. We then move from retirement to the pilgrim season, a time of great discovery.

CHAPTER SIX

Expecting the Worst

*If you bring forth what is inside you, what you
bring forth will save you. If you don't bring
forth what's inside you, what you don't bring
forth can destroy you.*

—The Gnostic Gospel of Thomas[1]

When counseling people about retirement, I often
ask them to talk about their fears. If they respond by
saying they have none, it usually indicates that they
are in complete denial or are terrible liars.

Retirement is a scary time, regardless of how
prepared we may think we are. It represents the
unknown and therefore a variety of fears and anxieties
seem to emerge. Karl Menninger, co-organizer of
the famous Menninger Clinic for the mentally ill,
has done a great deal of research in this area. He
said that fear is one of the earliest emotions a baby
experiences. Dr. Menninger has grouped early childhood fears into three categories: fear of falling, fear
of loud noises or catastrophe, and fear of abandonment.[2] As we grow older and more sophisticated,
Menninger states, these three categories are translated into adult versions. The fear of falling becomes

fear of failing or losing one's place in the job market. Fear of catastrophe becomes the fear of a crippling illness, and the fear of abandonment becomes fear of the loss of esteem or the loss of creativity.

These same fears often are expressed in retirement, but with slightly different emphasis. The fear of falling is translated in terms of separation. People begin to voice this when they ask: "What will happen when we no longer have a job to go to?" Fear of loud noises is translated into the fear of being seen as old and sickly. People often say: "I'm not sure I have saved enough. What happens if my health deteriorates and I can't take care of myself?" And finally, the fear of abandonment is transposed into the fear of isolation when business or professional associations are seen as a part of the past. Newly retired people often say: "We will no longer have any friends."

When contemplating retirement, it is easy to succumb to these fears, particularly when we have an understanding of life that is influenced by scarcity. Scarcity in terms of relationships, as well as resources, is what often brings us to the feeling that retirement is a state to be avoided at all costs. This real or imagined specter has the power to dominate many of our thoughts on retirement. In the process of counseling, people often express their fears by asking something like: "What if I don't have enough resources?" These feelings of scarcity are often what trigger our most basic anxieties.

Let me share how this fear has made contact in

my life. It is a common nightmare that many preachers have. In my dreams, it is Sunday morning, and as I walk to the pulpit the congregation begins to laugh. I don't see myself, but as I begin to preach, I suddenly realize that I am naked. Now this has nothing to do with nudity or lack of clothing. Nakedness in my dream represents my fear of deprivation, of being caught with nothing to say, of finding myself without notes in the pulpit. Nakedness ultimately represents my fear of scarcity. My dream tells me that my creative juices will dry up and I will have nothing left to say in the pulpit. Let me tell you, that is a nightmare that really produces night sweats for many clergy.

A friend who was in the twilight of life phoned me, and during our conversation he said: "All I've ever wanted from retirement is a little peace and security, a little tranquility, a time when we can rest and put aside our fears." It sounds so easy, but life doesn't usually work quite that way. One thing we know for certain is that life doesn't stand still. The experience of most of us is that just when you think you're ready for the "Golden Years," everything seems to turn to dust. Just as you have retirement all figured out, everything changes, old fears re-emerge, and scarcity becomes a framework for your life.

The best thing I could come up with for my friend was: Instead of seeking directly for tranquility, begin to believe that you live in the world of plenty rather than the land of scarcity. In the world of plenty there is enough for everyone, and the so-called necessary losses that come with retirement are easily met with new opportunities. This is particularly so when one views the transition as a pilgrimage, because pilgrims are enabled to view hardships differently. They see losses as messages to let go and move in a new direction.

Marcus Aurelius said in his stoic writings that the wise person is the one who has ceased "to be whirled around by external determinates."[3] Wisdom arises at that moment in a pilgrimage when you cease thinking in terms of deprivation, when you cease permitting your fears to pull you in every direction, when you cease letting yourself be jerked around by feelings of scarcity, when you can travel the inward road of abandonment. This then can turn our paths of discovery into a sacred journey.

But this is so much easier said than done. We live in a world where diminishment seems to be the order of the day. We are at best fragile people who are vulnerable to all sorts of losses and the fear of being subject to these losses is always in our subconscious. Courage is not ignoring the fear so much as not allowing it to color your whole existence. Courage is keeping your eyes focused on the journey and not on the many obstacles you may encounter. Courage is the ability to look at the many snarls we encounter through the eyes of a pilgrim and somehow find the ability to move into a new future rather than be stuck in the past.

Someone once said: "An ounce of experience is worth a pound of theory."[4] My experience has been that the expectation of scarcity and decline often become self-fulfilling prophecies. The more we give in to these basic fears that stem from early childhood emotions, the more we are likely to look on retirement as a stage in life to be avoided.

But the more we live in anticipation of a bright future, the more we are likely to look on retirement with a sense of hope. Jesus said it so well. Here is the "good news" to those of us retiring: "I have come," he said, "that you may have life, and have it more abundantly."[5]

Like it or not, deny it or not, this is an opportunity for pilgrimages where we can view change as part of an exciting transition into a world of abundance. Abundance, not scarcity, is our hope. This is the good news for those in the pilgrim season.

As mentioned earlier, I interviewed a number of people in the preparation of this book. One person was Fred, a gentleman who had a distinguished career in science before retirement. He worked on the Manhattan Project during World War II and was involved in space exploration as well as developing curriculum for the National Science Foundation. At the time of his retirement he was a professor at a university in the Midwest.

Fred explained that more than 20 years earlier, he had a problem with his voice. His vocal chords were blocked, and after an operation he was able to speak, but unable to lecture, so he took early retirement. With this transition in his life, he could have viewed his world as one of scarcity.

About the same time, Fred signed up for a beginners evening course in weaving at the local YMCA. "I was curious how a loom could produce such beautiful designs. How could such a simple machine make such a wide variety of textiles? I became more and more fascinated and also more skilled.

"At first it was a hobby, but then I began to see the mathematical relationship in design and symmetry, and I was able to bring in my scientific background. It was more of a shift from chemistry to weaving, but many of the elements of my former life are still there. I teach; I publish; I mentor people; just as I did before. I'm primarily a problem solver. I spend a lot of time researching new techniques, and then write them up and put the information on my webpage."

When asked what he missed of his former life, he answered: "I probably miss the contacts I had with my colleagues [the most]. I rarely see the people with whom I used to work, but things happen very rapidly in science. You can be out of it rather quickly unless you're willing to read the scientific journals and go to scientific meetings. When I look at my university peers, there are several patterns that emerge when they retire. Some move away to warm places and play golf, but many just move back after a few years. Others stay on and do roughly the same thing they always did: research, consulting, or advising.

Many who have tried this are floundering. They haven't found a strong focus to replace what they had been doing for 30 or 40 years. I was lucky; I found that new focus."

Fred now finds himself involved with weaving on a seven-day-a-week schedule. He puts on seminars and publishes books on weaving. He did not expect the worst when he retired, and it could be that he has found the best. Certainly in looking around his home at the beautiful examples of his weaving, his transition to retirement seems to have taken him to a world of beautiful abundance.

CHAPTER SEVEN

I'm Too Young for This

Do not go gentle into that good night. Old age should burn and rage at the close of day; Rage, rage against the dying of the light.

—Dylan Thomas[1]

You can deny it; you can bury it, and you can siphon it off. Some people get sick over it, and some even die from it. Anger: it's a common emotion to all human beings. I would speculate it is even more common to those who are retiring.

For most of us, anger is just there. It's neither good nor bad. The issue in retirement is how much this common emotion sets the agenda for our future. How much do we allow this anger to shape our identity?

The other day, while watching two younger people play a fast game of tennis, feelings of anger seemed to arise. Why was it that these two could move so gracefully, and I, with my worn-out knees, stumbled around like a wounded tank? It just wasn't fair.

At a recent church service, the clergy conducting the liturgy were doing a sloppy job. A thought went through my head. Why didn't they invite me to help? My resentment increased at not being able to conduct the service. Feelings of being put on the shelf overwhelmed me.

Today, I caught myself wishing I were in my 50s. Somehow this body of mine, along with the culture, has conspired to render me obsolete. Everywhere I turned there seemed to be signs saying: If you're over 65, you're over the hill.

In the *Odyssey*, Homer tells how the Greek general, Ulysses, was leading his army toward Troy. Unexpectedly, he came across a flooded river. His men were unable to cross because the river was too deep and too swift. Ulysses was so angered by this obstacle that he literally waded out up to his knees and thrashed the water with chains and then retired to his tent. I know that feeling. I've been there also. Anger, frustration, and resentment all bring about the feelings of wanting to retire into our tents.

Road rage is a term that has slipped into our vocabulary during the last decade or so. It refers to a feeling that comes over us when driving a car. It usually emerges when another driver frustrates us beyond what might be termed normal discourtesy.

Related to this is a new term, retirement rage. This is when our age interferes with our future, when we refuse to accept what is, and we lack a vision of what could be. Retirement rage is a spiraling downward process, where our perspective becomes distorted and we spew forth out of control.

In a classic scene of retirement rage, Norman, played by Henry Fonda in the movie, *On Golden Pond*, yells at Billy, the young boy who has come to visit.[2] Katharine Hepburn, who plays Fonda's wife in the movie, tells the boy that Norman wasn't yelling at him; he was yelling at life. She goes on to explain that sometimes you have to look hard at a person and remember he is trying to find his way—he is angry with himself and his condition.

In the early stages of retirement, anger is usually directed at those who contributed to the decision to retire: the boss, company regulations, fellow workers, or the culture. Some of this anger can be reality based, and some is simply characterized by a blaming of others. The problem is that as our anger recedes, the next emotion is a feeling of being victimized. We move from "Damn it, I'm mad at…" to "Woe is me. They're out to get me."

Whenever we slip into the role of a victim, we endeavor to make retirement at least partially the responsibility of others.

The victim role is often a warning that retirement rage has overcome the sense of reality. Acting like a victim is one way to avoid not coming to terms with our limitations. But the cost of not taking responsibility for our stage in life means that we limp into retirement with less energy and an unrealistic picture of who we are.

Anger also has a way of spreading. It can move quickly from what is happening on the outside to focusing on our insides. Anger, when turned inward in this way, usually leads to depression. This is a common issue for those who have recently retired. Signs that this anger has spread inward include an inability to sleep for more than a few hours at a time, feelings of worthlessness, and an overemphasis on the small irritants of normal living. Depression also can have physical manifestations. Some people who are retired begin to speak of extreme tiredness even after having six or seven hours sleep; constant back-aches, despite not doing any extra exercise, and general feelings of edginess or restlessness, even when there doesn't seem to be any real stress.

"But wait," you might be saying, "what of normal anger?" A number of years ago, psychologist George Bach and Peter Wyden wrote a book entitled, *The Intimate Enemy: How to Fight Fair in Love and Marriage*.[3] The book described work at their California-based institute, where they taught couples to have better fights. The institute primarily offered marriage counseling, but many of the findings are easily transferable to the retirement scene. Their premise is that anger is a normal part of relationships and can be creatively used. They say that few of us know how to use our anger, and we are chronically anxious about it getting out of hand. Therefore, we often deny that anger is present. "Who? Me angry? Never have I spoken a word in anger." And thus we kid ourselves that this emotion is not a part of our lives. Anger does not simply go away. If we deny it, anger will find a place to reside, either in our behavior or in our bodies.

The Bach-Wyden book suggests that anger is always present within intimate relationships and can be used in positive ways. Anger also can do two things for us. First, it can tell us something about ourselves that we usually try to ignore. And second, when acknowledged, it can draw us closer to those people who make up our support system.

Using the insights from the book, there are two steps we might take when we become aware of our anger in retirement. First, we have to recognize why we are angry, and then we have to be willing to put that anger aside after a small amount of time. This second step is by far the hardest.

The first step is to openly acknowledge the anger within us. The longer we cap it off and seal it from the outside world, the more it festers and grows. The beginning of wisdom here is knowing and admitting to another that we often tap into a reservoir of anger that is universal. When we fail to recognize our own anger, we tend to focus on what others have done to us. We often then see ourselves as blameless, or as the innocent victim. Conversely, we often paint others as the devil incarnate.

There is, in the Episcopal wedding service, a prayer that asks of God: "Give them grace, when they hurt each other, to recognize and acknowledge their fault, and to seek each other's forgiveness and yours."[4] Acknowledging our own involvement is a way to expose the anger that often lies deep within us.

The second step is learning to give away our anger. This may sound simple, but it isn't as easy as it sounds. Giving away our anger means giving away the memory of whatever has made us angry. This is a most difficult skill to learn and takes lots of practice. It's somewhat like giving away a worn-out pair of shoes that you no longer wear. Some of us hold on to those shoes even if they are no longer useful or stylish.

Another way to visualize anger is that it is like a wound we have incurred. Some of us keep rubbing and picking at it so that it never heals. One way to handle this problem is learning to be generous. If one is to begin practicing generosity, the initial step is to start by giving things away. Eventually you may learn to give your anger away.

There's a wonderful image from Tibetan Buddhism. It's as if we are holding in front of us a steaming bowl filled with our anger. This anger builds and builds and builds. Then self-pity gets hold of us, and there is a split second in which we can choose either to hold it to us or give it away by pouring it into the earth or by giving it to God (whatever your faith may direct). It involves either letting it go or pouring it into ourselves so that it takes possession of us. It's at these moments that we choose to keep our anger or learn to be generous.

You can deny it. You can bury it. Some people

get sick over it, but the bottom line is that when you retire, expect to have anger. The question is: What do you do with the anger you feel?

CHAPTER EIGHT:

The Business of Busyness

*God grant me the serenity to accept the things I
cannot change, the courage to change the things
I can, and the wisdom to know the difference.*

—Serenity Prayer[1]

The reasons people write books are quite varied.
Some write to earn a living; some write because they
have a need to express themselves, and some write
just to find out what they are thinking. I'm usually
in the latter group. It's difficult for me to articulate
my feelings at any given moment or in conversation. Usually, I think of the appropriate rejoinder in
the middle of the night. And my best ideas come to
me while I'm standing in the shower. That's why
it's important for me to get up early in the morning,
have a cup of coffee, and sit with a blank piece of
paper in front of me.

Soon after I retired, on one of those early mornings of reflection, I recall all the advice received in
the days before retirement. My friends who were
already into retirement often predicted an increase
in activity. "You'll begin to wonder," they said, "how
you ever found time to work."

Underlying these words is a belief system, sometimes referred to as the "protestant work ethic." It tells us that to be truly satisfied we must keep constantly busy.

It is surprising the time and energy retired people put into golf, tennis, bridge, and a host of other hobbies. It's almost as if they see time as a great vacuum that has to be filled with a variety of activities, lest someone accuse them of sloth. It seems as if this frenetic quest for filling up our days comes from a fear that we appear unproductive. It almost seems as if we have to constantly justify our existence by appearing busy.

I want to say to all my well-meaning friends who advise me that "busyness" is the key to retirement, that I'm a human being and not a human doing. In other words, "workaholism" may be seen as a virtue in our culture, but I consider it to be a disease that retirement can cure, not foster.

When contemplating the pilgrim season, those writers who pursue quietness and simplicity as a way of life seem closer to the mark. One of my favorite books is a small but significant one that Thomas Kelly wrote many years ago. It is titled *Testament of Devotion*.[2] It speaks eloquently of impoverished lives that result from an overabundance of things to do.

Kelly meant that by trying to embrace too many possibilities at once, a person could become impoverished. It is like sitting down to a rich meal and overeating. When this happens, the very food that tasted so good can make you sick. Kelly was suggesting that we could gorge ourselves with too many activities, just as we can overeat. The result of this overactivity is a sickness of the spirit.

David Ford, a British theologian at Cambridge, has labeled our age "The Age of *Overwhelmedness*." He says that we constantly take on so many burdens and keep busy with so many projects that we are permanently overwhelmed. In the years following retirement it is easy to have so many irons in the fire that none is able to glow. Over activity can easily produce a sickness in the spiritual sense.

Meister Eckhart, the 14th century mystic wrote about the "true poverty." He recommended that we empty ourselves of the need to be busy so that we could be free to wait in the moment. It was, he said, the highest way of being.

The secret of the pilgrim season, some have said, is learning to give ourselves permission not to do things and letting things happen. This is action through non-action. This cuts across the grain for many of us who have grown up with the 11th commandment, "Thou shalt not waste time," or with its corollary, "Waste not, want not." The great sin here seems to be not putting time to use.

But suppose we thought of time the way a pilgrim does. The art of a pilgrimage is to take time seriously. Time for the pilgrim is a gift from God and not a commodity to be used. Time as a gift can be savored, nurtured, and enjoyed. It can even be legitimately placed in the non-use category. As a gift freely given, without any strings attached, we can waste it or even throw it away. What pilgrims learn is the way to expend time without counting its cost.

I asked a retired friend recently what he does with his time each day. "I haven't quite gotten to the point," he said, "that I can give myself permission to do nothing all day, therefore I try to accomplish one thing each day." That has a good ring to it. It seems like the first step in simplifying life.

Another retired person said, "I try to sort out what is really important and only do those things that are utterly necessary."

Anne Lamont, in her book, *Tender Mercies*[3] tells of watching a movie about Gypsies. She was particularly taken by some of the older people. Her words are applicable to all that contemplate retirement. "It's a time for all those long deep breaths, time to watch more closely, time to enjoy what I've always been afraid of—the ease of understanding that life is not about doing. The Gypsies understood this. It is a time to get much less done, a time for all those holy moments."

The business of busyness is for an earlier stage of life. The pilgrim season is a time of appreciation, of holy moments, and of seeking what is special in our fast-paced lives. May we give ourselves permission to let go of things and find the wisdom to know the difference between what is urgent and what is simply a form of busyness.

CHAPTER NINE

How Quickly
We Are Forgotten

The moment of the rose and the moment of the yew tree are of equal duration.

—T.S. Eliot[1]

I guess I should not have been surprised. I was at a party some six months after I retired and ran into a peripheral member of my former congregation. I had spent a great deal of time counseling his wife through several traumatic experiences. After a few pleasantries I must have said something about missing the parish. "Oh," he replied, "were you the rector there very long?"

"More than 20 years," I answered, and then I was unable to keep my feelings from leaking out. "I guess you hadn't heard that I had retired," I said. "To tell the truth," he replied, "I never noticed."

Several years ago, a woman shared with me a story about her father. He had been head of a large manufacturing company in the '60s and '70s. He led the company for more than 20 years through some very rough economic times. When he retired, the company was in the best financial position that it had ever been. A few years later, her father died. Shortly thereafter, the woman visited the home office of the company and was shocked that no one remembered much about her father. "It was as if he had never been there," she reported.

A friend of mine in the social service field had worked seven days a week and about 15 hours a day in his career. His phone at work was never silent. After 30 years in one community, he decided to retire, but his worry was what would happen to the people who depended upon him. Three years after retirement the very few times his phone rings is when some salesperson calls.

We live in a culture that has often been characterized as "the Kleenex® culture." We are the first generation to believe that everything in life is disposable, to be used and then thrown away. How quickly we are forgotten.

When questioned, most people who have stopped working for a living likely would express the hope that they would be remembered for their contributions. Lurking in the background is the dread that their efforts during the working years will be dismissed as unimportant or forgotten. The fact is that life moves on, and the contributions we make are often forgotten, or, if not forgotten, at least put aside so that new participation may flourish.

There are some organizations that give a retiring person the title *emeritus*. Basically this means that the retired person has been honorably discharged from active duty, but is still retained on the rolls. It is a way to recognize the contribution of the person and an attempt to insure that the memory of the person is not completely forgotten.

The sentiment is to be applauded, but the title is often misunderstood and doesn't usually add to the life of the organization. It is not my purpose to denigrate titles. They are important tools for solidifying our identity. Yet *emeritus* as a title often leaves the person in a never-never land where one's still a part of the former work life, but not fully.

I believe it is important for the retired person to face into the reality of his or her new stage. Contrary to much popular wisdom, I would suggest resisting whatever seems to deny the fact of retirement, whether it is a title or one of the more popular roles, such as continuing as a consultant. Not that there are not some legitimate exceptions, but the problem with these titles is that they have a tendency to allow one to hold on even after retirement. The work of retirement is the realization that the past is past.

The process of being forgotten, painful as it may be, is almost a necessity for the life of an organization; particularly so, if it is to move from dependence on former leaders to growth and independence. We might even speculate that forgetting is a function of renewal. Instead of looking backward, renewed organizations are able to put aside the past and keep focused on the future.

This is not advocating that organizations cast away their corporate memories. They need to remember the lessons they have learned from the important figures in their past. It is only in remembering that we can prevent making many of the mistakes of the past. Reinventing the wheel wastes a lot of time and leads to corporate exhaustion. The key here is that although individuals who have retired may be forgotten, it's important to retain the insights that have been of importance over the years.

The Old Testament book, Ecclesiastes, accurately describes the feelings of someone who looks over his accomplishments and realizes how quickly it all is forgotten. The writer of this book is referred to as "the preacher." In essence, thoughts voiced by the preacher may be summarized as: "I consider all that my hands had done, and the toil I spent doing it, all to be vanity, and a chasing after the wind. There is nothing to be gained under the sun."[2]

There stands the poster boy for the age of depression. Can't you just imagine that he has recently retired and is looking around for some signs of appreciation for what he has contributed? Instead he finds his former organization to have corporate amnesia. There is no memory of what he accomplished. The 10, or 20, or 30 years seem to have vanished, and former fellow-employees act as if he never was a part of the organization. It all seems reasonable to declare: All is vanity and chasing after the wind.

I wonder if the writer of Ecclesiastes doesn't speak for many who have recently retired. The hard lesson in retirement is that much of what we have done will soon be forgotten.

A friend, who retired a few years ago, was visiting us during one holiday season. In the course of our conversation, I asked: "What do you want for Christmas?" What do you give to someone who seems to have everything that money can buy? "Is there something you need?" I asked.

"Yes," she replied, "I seem to have misplaced some of the good memories of my past life, and my former colleagues seem to have forgotten me."

I began to ask myself, "How do you bundle up a bunch of memories?" And then it came to me. Why not make a scrapbook of all the accomplishments, something to pass on to one's children. This scrapbook becomes a sacred symbol of your past life. Its sacredness comes through your intention to pass it on to future generations. Whenever future generations open this book, those who are closest to you will share a small part of your journey.

The purpose of this chapter has been to raise these questions: What parts of your past working life would you put into a scrapbook? What deserves to be remembered as something that will endure the indignity of time?

Let's not minimize the pain and the sense of loss that happens when we are forgotten. For many, it feels as if we have been rendered invisible. This can be a chilling realization. People's memories, at best, are short-lived, and the hurt of being forgotten can be difficult for our egos to handle.

And yet, as we reflect on our past, isn't it more important in the grand scheme of things to have impacted the lives of people than to be remembered for specific accomplishments? Some years ago a survey was taken of people living in retirement homes. They were asked what they would do differently if they could go back and do it all over again. The replies fell into three main categories. First, they wished they had loved more. Second, they wished they could have followed their hearts instead of their heads. And third, that those close to them would remember what they had accomplished.

CHAPTER TEN

Well, Dear, What Are We Doing Today?

To survive is important, but to thrive is elegant...

—Maya Angelou[1]

I sometimes wish I had never heard the familiar phrase that comes at the end of so many fairy tales: "and they lived happily ever after." In most fairy tales there is conflict, action, and resolution. Then we are presented with: "and they lived happily ever after."

The reason is, this idyllic image distorts our image of later life. Does retirement mean simply living happily ever after? We often have the illusion that the first 65 years were the difficult years, the times of growth and change. Then we come to a certain age called retirement and life becomes simpler.

This kind of thinking is setting us up for disappointment and disillusionment. Real life is not like a fairy tale. There are no points beyond which struggle and change are not a part of the mix, but how we handle these changes and obstacles plays a major role. Among those interviewed for this book was

Bill, a park development director before he retired. Prior to that, he had retired from the military after 25 years of service.

After retirement from two careers, he explained that his financial and family obligations had been completed. "We weren't rich, but we were O.K," he said, "and each of the kids had money for their first year in college. I was open to something new, and for me it meant travel. I was in my 50s and could still go out and do it."

Bill's wife had other thoughts. During the time he was traveling in the military she had joined a church that had different beliefs than the one previously attended. "She had become oriented toward this new church philosophy and wanted to remain in our old community; I wanted to travel," he said. As a result, they divided everything they owned and divorced.

So often we are told that retirement is about stopping work and taking it easy. To Bill, taking it easy was not what retirement was all about. Although he was in the pilgrim season, he felt his inner journey could only be successful in physical travel. His retirement meant choosing a new way of life.

His new life included Susan, whom he met while taking a course at a local community college. They were married, and Bill's travel dreams came true. "We put everything we owned in storage and traveled around the world for two years, spending three months in New Zealand, six months in Australia, and some time in Bali, Indonesia, Malaysia, South America, Japan, and South Africa. It was perfectly wonderful."

Since that time, Bill and Susan bought an RV and have been traveling around the United States. "I think we've basically become gypsies," he said.

The great problem with the years following work is that suddenly many of the old comfortable routines are disrupted or completely swept away. In a twinkling of the eye the motivation as well as the pattern of arising at a certain hour is gone. There is no need to be fully dressed, shaved, or to eat at an appointed hour. During earlier times, even routines that were most disliked had their place.

Bill and Susan believed that living in a house makes people overly scheduled. They found that life in an RV offered them a spontaneity that doesn't come with a house. They don't go to specified locations every year. "We're the traveling kind, a new experience every day," Bill said. "We are interested in exploring places, seeing new sights, and meeting new friends. We hope to continue this lifestyle until we're too old to move around or too broke and have to settle down and make money."

Bill and Susan are on a journey. The word journey in its original context refers to the distance one could travel in a day. The journey for Bill and his new wife becomes a pilgrimage as they discover that the distance traveled is less important than the experience gained.

Shortly after I retired, my wife or I would often turn to the other at breakfast and say, "Well, what's our agenda today?" The question became old very quickly. The sense of freedom in retirement was exhilarating. The feeling of having the time to waste was refreshing, but the necessity to plan one's day, to apportion one's time, to realize the importance of each moment, was at best draining. It seemed as if every day our plans would go awry and something more important arose in the middle of our best-laid plans.

After a while we sat down and asked ourselves what routines were important and what could be discarded. What new routines needed to be established? What was it that nurtured our souls and contributed to our sense of meaning? What routines from our old life were simply vestiges continued for appearance sake? Another way to ask the question is: "What patterns were life-giving, and what patterns had lost their meaning through the years?" This process of raising questions is of particular importance to those who see their journey as a pilgrimage.

As we reflected together in our new life, we chose consciously to initiate certain routines, certain predictable patterns that we both could count on. Once we had established the routines, then the daily schedule began to take shape. We were able to figure out when we were making schedules and when schedules were making us. It became clearer as to what agendas were demanding of our attention, and what tended to erode our souls.

We all have a need for routines, a need to follow certain set procedures; to behave in expected ways. It is this predictability that grounds us to reality. We might even say that routines are necessary for our survival as human beings. They are one way that we can count on each other for certain behaviors. Another justification for routines is that they can help to solidify relationships. It is important for those who are closest to us to anticipate our movements.

Routines within themselves are a neutral activity. They are neither good nor bad, neither life-enhancing nor death-dealing. The absence of routines, though, can often lead us down a path characterized by chaos. Some personality types can live with uncertainty and even welcome a certain degree of chaos; most of us have a need for routines that support us and upon which we can count.

The secret of retirement is not that life continues in an unbroken pattern, or that we will simply "live happily ever after." The secret is the understanding that in each stage we will be asked to establish patterns. Do not ask: "What routines are expected?" or "What patterns are normal?" Instead, ask: "What makes me come alive?" And then ask: What furthers intimacy with the special people in your life?" What the world needs are more alive people. What we need are closer relationships in this stage of our pilgrimage.

One of the persons interviewed about retirement said that he and his wife set aside a couple of hours every week, if not more often, to talk about what's going on in their inner lives. "We call it 'driving a wedge in the week.' Nothing can interrupt this time, no calls from kids, no grocery shopping," he said.

Another described retirement as a new experience, in that he's planning his own day-to-day life, rather than catering to a schedule that's set by someone else. "I think I'm happier than I've ever been," he said. "I think I'm more relaxed. I know I'm happier with myself."

CHAPTER ELEVEN

It's Nice to Know Where You're Going

"When a man leaves home, he leaves some scrap
of his heart. Is that not so? It's the same with
a place a man is going to," he [Godric] said.
"Only then he sends a scrap of his heart ahead."

—Frederick Buechner[1]

As a child, I was a voracious reader of the Uncle Wiggley series. Uncle Wiggley was an amazing rabbit that used to go off on adventures. These expeditions were called, "Funny Bone Hikes." The essence of a funny bone hike was that you never planned ahead and therefore you never knew where the journey would end. In later years it was easier to understand that Uncle Wiggley was the stuff of stories, and in real life we need to plan ahead.

The Roman philosopher Seneca, in reference to the shortness of life, once wrote: "A sailor without a destination has trouble knowing a good wind from an ill wind." If we paraphrase this wisdom we might say: "A person who is in the pilgrim stage of life and has not planned ahead has trouble knowing where he or she is, at any given moment."

There are those types who don't believe in making plans. They have decided to "go with the flow." "Qué sera, sera" (whatever will be, will be) may have been a good song for Doris Day in the 1950s, but it makes little sense as we move into retirement.

So why does planning for retirement seem frightening to many people? Why is it that we put off planning ahead for this important stage of life? Is it because of our anxiety over the unknown future?

There is a whole section in the British Museum in London that traces the history of map-making. Some of the maps are more than 4,500 years old. One of the more interesting points of those ancient maps is the way they depicted the areas that had not been charted. Instead of leaving those spaces blank, or simply acknowledging that this territory was yet to be explored, these ancient mapmakers filled these areas with images of dragons and monsters and wild beasts. These fanciful illustrations represented their apprehension of the unknown. Let's be honest, most of us feel a sense of unease regarding the not-yet parts of our lives, and it is thus easier to put off planning for the future in retirement.

Most of us realize that the process of planning is the only way we can have some control over the future. Yogi Berra, the former New York baseball player/philosopher is reported to have said: "If you don't know where you're going, you'll likely end up someplace else." Even though we are anxious about the unknown, deep down we know that Yogi was probably right.

In pursuing the thoughts about planning in retirement, I met Ralph, a vigorous looking man in his 60s. He was tanned, appeared to be fit, and his handshake and whole demeanor was of a self-assured, successful businessman. He had retired a few years earlier from his own construction firm.

Ralph had been building up his company for 18 years, he said. "Along the way my son joined me, and after a while I decided he was ready to take over. The time came in November, and I said to myself: 'Ralph, there is no turning back.' This was a little scary, because I didn't know how my son would do. It probably was scarier for my wife," he grinned, "because all of a sudden I was going to be in her world, trying to run things at home like I've been accustomed to in business. That really bothered her."

Thus, Ralph set down his plan: "In my structured way, I tried to lay out how many hours a week I would allocate to doing things with family, playing golf, traveling, and being active in the community. There were three community organizations on which I focused my time and energy.

"When I was working for a living, I was married to my job. When you don't have the business to worry about, you can replace it with other things. I've done that by concentrating on the church. My timing has been good. I've been able to provide some of the thoughts from the business world in working with the church."

In spite of his planning, Ralph has encountered some problems. "I've had a hard time trying to break some old habits. I haven't done a good job of saying: 'O.K., it's all right to relax. You don't have to manage things anymore.' I've got too darn much going on. There's no time for me to sit back and relax. But how do you say no to those community organizations to which you've committed yourself?"

Ralph does find benefit in working as a volunteer in the community, compared to his work before retirement. "I'm more relaxed as I serve the community. The sense of urgency in the business world is gone. I am able now to step back and say 'Wait a minute. Why are we having to hurry into this?'"

He finds another merit in his community volunteering: "I can offer my best thoughts, and if they don't accept them, they can fire me. It isn't the end of the world. So it's a whole different mindset. I think it makes the retirement years more fun."

There are some dos and don'ts in planning for retirement. Let me describe how the process of planning can be done. First, sit down in a quiet spot with a pen and paper, and begin to fantasize about the future. What will it look like a few years from now? How will you feel? Begin to focus on some goals similar to a navigator about to embark on a long voyage. Imagine that you are leaving for a journey from which you will not return. What do you need to do to prepare for this pilgrimage? At other times, you might imagine that God is talking and saying: "Now is the time to live your ideal life. What must you do?" The art of planning is the art of imagining how we would act if we were already involved in our journey.

During this first step, one must guard against that little voice inside that goes: "Come on, be practical, be a realist." This is the voice of doom. It will keep the planner earthbound. It's the voice that squishes our dreams and cuts us off from becoming the kind of person God wants us to be. It's the voice that tells us, "What you have is as good as it's going to get." Close the door and give a deaf ear to that voice. It sounds like a parent's voice that used to say, "That's just the way things are."

When you've finished the first step and have some really wonderful dreams, then come back to the present. Ask yourself the question: "What might I do in the present to make the pilgrimage possible?"

The chances are you will find that you're going to have to give up something for the pilgrimage. Maybe a lifestyle that you enjoyed, possibly some habits that gave you pleasure. Be prepared. But if this new stage is really to be a pilgrimage that is a sacred journey, then the giving up or letting go of things is very much part of the process. (The word *sacred* comes from the same Latin word *sacrifice*, to give up.) Without a sense of sacrifice, the pilgrimage is in danger of becoming just a casual, entertaining tour of an unfamiliar site.

Your imagined future may not be achieved. The plans you've jotted down may be scratched, changed, or, at best, put on hold. But this much is true. If you go through a process of planning for a pilgrimage, you will no longer settle for whatever seems to emerge. As you plan, you'll begin to see new options and the possibility of a different map for the retirement years.

And then somehow in the process, parts of your heart will be transferred into a more exciting future in this new stage of life. You will have started on the pilgrim season rather than moving grimily into the stage often called retirement.

CHAPTER TWELVE

There is No Such Thing as Retirement

I am tired of being
Tight, controlled,
Tensed against the invasion of novelty,
Armed against tenderness,
Afraid of softness.
I am tired of directing my world
Making
Doing
Shaping
God give me madness
That does not destroy
Wisdom
Responsibility
Love

—Sam Keen[1]

Quite often when asked to give a talk on religion and retirement, the invitation is rather vague. My experience has been that they are looking for a speaker to bless their present understandings of religion and retirement, and I hesitate to do that.

First, I hesitate because I can't find much help from Scriptures. I have searched the Bible from start to finish. I have pored through several learned commentaries, and I have never come across the word retirement. Even the thought of ceasing work seems foreign to the writers of the Bible.

Work, according to the Bible, was more of a sacred calling than a way to earn a living. Work was never seen as a 9-to-5 activity. It did not begin or end at a certain prescribed age. People were born into their jobs. Their work was inseparable from their very identity.

It wasn't until we moved from an agrarian economy to an industrial society that the workers' identities became separate from their vocations. It is interesting to note that when the disciples became Jesus' followers, they were still identified by their original work descriptions. The writers of the New Testament never referred to Peter as the "former" fisherman or to Luke as the "retired" physician. Once a fisherman, always a fisherman; once a doctor, always a doctor.

Second, I hesitate to accept these speaking engagements, because I don't relish making people feel uncomfortable. One of the major themes found throughout the Bible is growth. The great challenge for people of biblical faith is to keep growing wherever you find yourself in life. For many people, retirement is seen as a time to settle back and enjoy the so-called "Golden Years." This settling down is antithetical to biblical religion. Most groups that ask me to speak want comfort, not challenge—safety, not risk. If I were to say to them that there is no mistake more fatal than stopping to grow and settling for what is, they probably would not hear my words, and if they did, they would summarily reject my message.

And finally, I would hesitate to be a speaker because most groups want to know how to adjust to where they are, rather than finding new possibilities at their stage in life. We humans have a remarkable capacity to adapt to what is. We can lose a hand or a foot; we can lose a job or an income; we can lose most anything and somehow keep going as if nothing were wrong. But this talent also can keep us from expecting anything to change.

We all have learned to "make do." We wake up one morning and find we can't hear as well, we make do with what is left of our hearing capacity. We find we are no longer the sought-after consultants we once were, and we make do with what is left in life. There is something grand in this, but very often we forget that we need not simply adjust. There are other possibilities in retirement. We can change.

This is a difficult message to sell to groups, because it's so easy just to go along with what is. There is an old Yiddish saying: "To a worm in horseradish, the whole world is horseradish." That expression means: If we never imagine there are alternatives to our situations, then we assume that the way we are living is the only way. We then think that retirement always involves a loss of friends, a diminution of interest in the world, and a feeling of sitting on the shelf and watching the world go by.

There was no indication of such complacency in Tony, a retired army officer who I interviewed two years after his retirement. He had served in Vietnam and Korea during his 28 years of military duty. He and his family settled in a university town, where he took some classes to prepare him for teaching, and then became involved in volunteerism.

"I had heard a lot of stories about people retiring from the service and they seemed to just go to pot. Many of them became alcoholics, but I was pretty sure that I could exist 'on the outside,'" he said.

"I had been stationed here [the city of retirement] for three years while I was in the service," he said, "and we had made some good church friends."

Tony learned new skills in his volunteer work. "I've been very active in Habitat for Humanity. I've learned a lot about carpentry and house building from the people at Habitat." He used to volunteer about three days a week, but arthritis and what he termed "a nasty fall" reduced his involvement with Habitat to one day a week, but his volunteerism didn't stop there. He goes one day a week to the local community college to tutor students in math and help students with their homework. "Between tutoring and house building, I'm kept pretty busy," he said.

What we need are more positive examples, such as Tony, of people who have gone beyond the horse-radish stage.

Nadine Stair, who wrote, *If I Had My Life to Live Over*, is someone who has been able to take the risk of exploring other options. For some, her words are madness; for others, this is the hope of real sanity in a world that simply asks us to conform or to adjust to what is:

"If I had my life to live over, I'd try to make more mistakes. I would relax. I would limber up. I would be crazier. I would be less hygienic. I would take more chances. I would take more trips. I would climb more mountains, swim more rivers, watch more sunsets. I would burn more gasoline, eat more ice cream. I'd have more actual problems and fewer imaginary ones.

"I have been one of those people who doesn't go anywhere without a thermometer, a hot water bottle, a raincoat, and a parachute. If I had it to do over again, I would go places and do things and travel lighter. I'd ride more merry-go-rounds and pick more daisies."[2]

I don't know what Nadine Stair's age is, but I can only say: "Why not try? Why not picture the rest of your life as a pilgrimage and ride more merry-go-rounds and pick more daisies." All they can do is call you crazy.

CHAPTER THIRTEEN:

Withdraw From the World?

…When you finish with a job it is wiser to make the break completely. Cut off the old life, clean and sharp. If your mind is tired, that is the only way. If your mind is lively you will soon find other interests.

—Caroline Lejeune[1]

Several of us were sitting in a restaurant exchanging some thoughts about our lives. Across the table, a recently retired friend (we'll call him George), said: "I'll tell you what I've done. I've stopped reading all newspapers. I don't turn on the TV news, and I no longer listen to the radio." He said that when he was working, he would get up and, with his first cup of coffee, read the *Wall Street Journal*. Then with breakfast, he would turn on the radio to a well-known commentator.

"By the time I was having my second cup of coffee," he said, "I'd either be furious over all the pain, or thoroughly disgruntled with the human race."

Since his retirement he's taken a permanent sabbatical from the world's problems. "My blood pressure no longer rises," he said, "and I can enjoy breakfast with my wife in a more leisurely manner. The morning paper still is delivered, but now I just pick it up and throw it in the garbage can."

Perhaps George speaks for many who have retired. The temptation to withdraw, to cease caring, to blot out the disturbing aspects of the news is always present. If we succumb to the temptation, after a while, we forget whether we have withdrawn from the world or the world has withdrawn from us. George does not talk about how his withdrawal affects the rest of the world. Do his friends still enjoy being with him? Do his children and grandchildren still find him interesting or do they look at him with regret that they can no longer talk together about events in the world. George has isolated himself, and soon likely will find he is a boring individual, even to himself.

There is an illusion abroad. It may not be peculiar to retirees, but certainly it is fostered by the process of retirement. The illusion is that our behavior no longer matters to the rest of the world. Retirement is viewed by many as permission to cease caring. They no longer feel responsible for the rest of society. Their only concern is for maintaining their own sense of well-being.

Come to think of it, this is the same illusion people have when they double-park their cars, cheat on their income taxes, or pass homeless persons on the street. They convince themselves that what they are doing doesn't matter to other people. They delude themselves into assuming there is no connection between them and the rest of the world.

As far back as the story of Cain and Abel, we find people claiming no responsibility for what is happening around them. "Am I my brother's keeper?"[2] was the cry of Cain as he desperately tried to withdraw from the murder of his brother. But the answer to that question has always been a resounding "yes." It is an illusion to suppose we are not our brother's keeper. The truth of mutual responsibility has been the basis of common law, the foundation of all major religions, and at the heart of all moral and ethical teachings.

Jesus added a dimension of the sacred to this fact of relatedness to each other. In the well-known passage in the New Testament, Jesus passed judgment on those who withdrew from the needy. Those who chose to be bystanders to the world's pain responded to Him by asking: "When, Lord, did we see you hungry, or naked, or in prison?" And Jesus responded by telling them that all of humanity partakes of His sacred body. "Inasmuch as you have done it unto the least of these," He told them, "you have done it unto me."[3]

Not wanting to sound like a retired preacher, I recall trying to be a little subtler. I believe I tried to reply to George's statements in a non-judgmental way. I said, "I'm sure there is some relief in being able to turn off and tune out the world's problems, but if you cut yourself off from the problems, aren't you isolating yourself?"

His answer was a classic. "I prefer," he said, "the discomfort of isolation to the perils of feeling responsible for the messes of the world. After all, I'm now retired and I don't have to worry about anybody but myself."

George's problem is he mixed up two words, occupation and vocation. Occupation is what you do in life, your career, your job, the work you do from 9 to 5. Vocation, on the other hand, is who you are, your mission in life, your passion, or to use a word that is the Latin root of the word vocation, your "calling." Occupation usually ends at a certain age. We can retire from an occupation, but we cannot retire from our vocations. Vocations are for life.

Acceptance of this distinction suggests that although we all have different occupations, our vocations are all the same. The vocation of everyone is to connect, be concerned, and care for everything in this world of ours. In *The Color Purple*,[4] Celie, the young girl, expressed it so well when she said she knew her arm would bleed if she cut a tree. This sense of connection, of all living things being together in the same boat, is one way to see our vocation. The great task in retirement is to further our vocation at a time when our occupation has ceased to be a concern.

Erik Erikson suggested one further argument that might be used. In his book, *Childhood and*

Society, Erikson indicates that when we reach different stages of life, our concerns shift. As we become older, he writes, many of us gradually take on a consuming interest for oncoming generations. He calls this "generativity," the gift of caring for the good of those to come. "Individuals who do not develop generativity," Erikson warns, "often begin to indulge themselves as if they were their own one-and-only-child."[5]

Retirement is an excellent time to enter into that stage called "generativity." We now are afforded the time to get involved and to accept new challenges.

I know a man who had been a lawyer in a small Midwestern town. Let's call him Charles. He wasn't into causes; in fact, he wasn't involved in much of anything other than his own practice. When he retired, he planned to kick back, do a little traveling, and watch the younger people run the world.

Then one day he became a grandfather. At that point he began to think of the future beyond his own lifetime. He questioned what kind of a world there would be for his grandchild. Like the prodigal son in the Gospel,[6] "he came to himself." He began to be involved. Ecology no longer was just a word. Global warming was more than a concern of a few scientists. When someone cut down a tree in the rain forest, this retired man bled.

At a later time, Charles was interviewed by a local reporter who asked why he became so involved in these causes. His reply was: "When my family gathers for my funeral, I want them to know what tracks I blazed for others to follow."

Among retirees interviewed in preparing this book, was Sam, a salesman for 26 years. He didn't want the world to stop so he could get off. "I certainly don't feel that I have taken myself out of the world," he said.

He and his wife live in an upscale retirement community in southern Arizona. "We are so blessed that we can be in a place like this and do pretty much what we want to do. My volunteer work keeps me feeling that I am contributing something. I just feel that I am in another phase of my life.

"I've always tried to be open to people, but now I am more aware of the problems people have, what the differences are, and I am more at peace with the way I meet people. Before retirement, when I was in business, I wasn't satisfied with who I was. I think it has taken me 70 years to get here, but I'm a different person. Retirement years have given me some time to conquer what I had been too busy to look at. In a way I have had a sense of being reborn. I'm happier than I've ever been. I think I'm more relaxed. I know I'm happier with myself."

What a pity that George (mentioned at the beginning of this chapter) did not witness and experience some of the pleasures of retirement that Charles and Sam have found.

Every retiree is faced with the question of whether to seek ways to withdraw from the world or whether to look for ways to reach out for a better understanding of what the world is really about.

Could Charles and Sam be right? Rather than the end of life, is retirement an opportunity to be reborn?

CHAPTER FOURTEEN

Saying Hello and Goodbye

For the Garden is the only place there is, but you
 will not find it
Until you have looked everywhere and found
 nowhere that is not desert
The miracle is the only thing that happens, but
 to you it will not be apparent
Until all events have been studied and nothing
 happens that you cannot explain
And life is the destiny you are bound to refuse
Until you have consented to die.

—W.H. Auden[1]

Among the first gestures a baby learns is the wave of a hand, a signal that means "goodbye." Then shortly thereafter a child masters the way to say "hello." As adults, it is beneficial that we obtain an early start on the words hello and goodbye, because they represent our most basic task. From the very start of life to its conclusion, we humans are always involved in the process of ongoing goodbyes to the old and hellos to the new.

We have all heard of or known persons who are perpetual children, persons who have been unable to successfully say goodbye to adolescence and hello to a more adult way of thinking and acting. The ease in which we manage saying "goodbye" and "hello," enabling us to move from one stage of life to another, tells us a lot about who we are.

The way we say goodbye will be a major factor in determining how we enter into a new stage of life. Our hellos and goodbyes are important clues to our future. If one is unable to say goodbye, one can never fully go on a pilgrimage. This metaphor for a journey or a transition loses its meaning when we refuse to let go of our old life.

Many contemporary novelists remind us that we have to say goodbye to some things in order to say hello to others. Through the years we have developed patterns for saying hello and goodbye. These patterns are ways that we have developed that work for us. What is most interesting about these patterns is that they are relatively consistent and predictable, whether we are focusing on retirement, marriage, leaving a job, or attending a social engagement.

It has been suggested that if you want to find out how people will act as they move into retirement, simply look at how they handled themselves at a recent party. Observe them as they arrive and watch their behavior as they leave. You will be able to gain significant clues on how they move into the retirement stage. The way we say hello and goodbye in one situation is pretty consistent for all situations.

Over the years, there are basically three patterns

that people use to say goodbye. They correspond closely to personality types in the way they manage movement in other phases of their lives.

The first are labeled the "invisible persons." These people would rather leave a situation unnoticed and unmissed. They firmly believe that the test of a successful job is that after they leave, nothing changes. Throughout life they have gone out of their way not to encourage dependence upon themselves. They prefer to work behind the scenes and not take credit for things that happen. They avoid being the center of attention. In social situations they leave with the least amount of fuss. For this type, goodbyes are painful and they have learned to avoid acknowledging losses. Goodbyes seem to represent permanent breaks. It is easier for these persons to focus on the past than to deal with the present experience.

In the second category are the "highly visible" types. These people have high control needs. They attempt to tie up as many loose ends as possible. Saying goodbye is seen as an opportunity to confront, consolidate, and console as many parts of the system as possible. They firmly believe that there is an obligation to make sure the persons replacing them will appreciate all that has gone before and that they will be remembered for their direction. In a social situation these persons easily become the center of attention and rarely say goodbye until most people have left. Good-byes are only temporary inconveniences, and this type focuses mostly on the future.

In the final category are the "visible" types. These people are aware of the separation but are able to see it from both sides—the person leaving and the people left behind. This person understands that it is important to involve as many people as possible in creating and planning for transitions. Goodbyes then become community functions. Grief over leaving can be done openly and planned. The disruption of both the system and the individual who is leaving can be taken as a normal part of saying goodbye. The new situation on both sides can be met with anticipation and hope. This third type tends to encourage celebrations rather than focusing on the loss. In social situations this person attempts to make goodbyes a community focus and therefore would choose to leave when the greatest numbers are leaving. These persons usually focus on the present moment.

Whatever type you find yourself to be—invisible, highly visible, or visible—the same issues are present at retirement. The principal task is how do you say goodbye without having to hold tightly to what has been and then how do you allow yourself to say hello to the new stage. For some of us, it seems almost impossible to detach from those parts of our daily work life that have given us a measure of security. Detaching is one of the most difficult tasks that we have in retiring. Some never are able to accomplish this task.

In speaking with a woman who recently mentioned how difficult it is to be a member of Alanon[2], she said it is much easier to be a part of Alcoholics Anonymous (AA). To join AA, all you have to do is have a desire to stop drinking, but to become a member of Alanon you have to be ready to give up all kinds of things. In addition to stopping the enabling of another person, you have to stop rescuing and avoid triangulating and a host of behaviors that have become second nature. And added to all that, she said, you have to detach with love.

I'm not sure why it is, she said, but I personally like to hold on to things. Detaching from anything—from a car to a job—makes me anxious. Goodbyes do not come easily, but this much I have learned: Unless we can say goodbye, we will never be able to say hello. We begin learning this art as an infant and continue to refine our skills throughout our lifetimes.

The retirement stage of life isn't easy. There is always a sense of loss. The trick is learning to detach with a sense of grace. Instead of simply grieving for all that you have lost, here is a different strategy: Learn to enjoy what you have left.

A Jewish mystical text says: "At the last judgment, God will ask us, 'Why didn't you enjoy all the good things in life that were permitted to you, instead of wishing for all the things you didn't have?'"

One interview for this book was with John, a

retired university professor. As we sat in his living room, he posed these questions: "What's the best time to retire? What's a good time to get out?" Then, he answered himself: "Before things get to the point of difficulty or boredom. I didn't want to just hang around the house. I had to figure out how I could live and exist in my wife's workplace, because she runs a business out of our home.

"I have a colleague at the university who retired and just goes down to the office everyday and sits and reads. I couldn't do that. I think he goes down there because he doesn't have anything else to do. My father, who lived to age 99, could never say goodbye to his university position. He kept going back, visiting old colleagues, writing and giving talks even when he became blind.

"There was a lot of anxiety when I first started thinking about retirement. I was worried about what I was going to do. How could I be useful? I could picture myself just walking around the house and watching TV. I have always been active, and this seemed like the end of the world. There was also the fear of the unknown.

"But I have found that retirement is a 'letting go' experience. I think of it as a weaning. My wife is one who says, 'I don't want to ever look back,' and I have found that it's important to keep focused on the future."

For many of us, retirement allows us to say hello to the new and frees us to say goodbye to the old.

The pilgrim season is not a time of doing things to make money or be judged successful. It's a time to say hello to new challenges just because they are there.

CHAPTER FIFTEEN

It's Monday Morning

Here on the pulse of this new day
You may have the grace to look out
Into your sister's eyes and into your brother's face
And say simply, with hope, Good Morning.
To look up and out
Brothers, face your country.

—Maya Angelou[1]

It is Monday morning and the juices begin to flow. You are like an old racehorse that hears the bell and begins to paw the ground and edges to the starting gate. For years Monday has represented the day you get started. For most people, whatever their work has been, Monday mornings have been the time for speculating on the week ahead—laying plans, making decisions—plotting the future.

It was not too long ago when, waking on a Monday morning, I found myself asking questions.

First, "What will I do with this five-day block of time?"

Then, "In retirement, is one day any different from another?"

Finally, pulling the covers over my head, I asked, "Why should I even get out of bed this morning?"

These morning musings, not particularly profound, can produce a sense of disorientation to the newly retired. For years we have shaped our lives around the calendar. As a priest, Sunday was a big day for me. Now it is simply a day to read the papers and attend a service at church. For most people, Monday is start-up time and Friday is wind-down time. The weekdays are for work; the weekends are for play. One set of clothes for working and another set for fun and games. What happens when the boundaries are no longer as clear—when Monday is no different from Saturday?

For some, there is a great letdown. No longer are we dependent on our alarm clocks. "Alleluia," we say to ourselves. "We have been delivered from the burden of being a clock-watcher." But before our rejoicing is complete, we have to inquire deliverance from what? In the back of our minds we wonder if this kind of freedom is simply setting us adrift in a sea of meaningless moments. Are we now forced to create our own calendars? The ethos of work no longer shapes our understanding of time. Even the most common of habits—sitting down to three meals a day—at a certain point is called into question.

Many retirees recount the incredible feeling of freedom when they were able to say: "I will eat when I'm hungry, not when it's lunchtime. I will play when I want and not wait until the weekend arrives." This new-found freedom can be a blessing for some, but for others it feels like an unwanted burden.

One of my favorite comic strips is "Garfield," the cat.[2] A few years ago, the creator, Jim Davis, depicted Garfield as a freedom fighter with a bandana around his head. We see him zipping through a pet shop at night opening all the cages. As he opens them, he yells, "You're free, you're free!" The next panel shows all the animals cowering in their cages and not moving out. Garfield stops and says: "Huh, so you're not into freedom." The final panel has Garfield running through the shop closing all the cages and shouting, "You're secure, you're secure!" Cartoonist Davis is making a significant point. Many people are prepared to trade freedom for security and predictability. For some, cages are not all that bad.

The challenge of retirement is finding the courage to go beyond the cages of yesterday. Shortly before retirement, I ran into a bit of wisdom. It came from, of all places, the divorce recovery program that was meeting at our parish. On the blackboard in one of the meeting rooms, someone had written these words: "If you always do what you've always done, you will always get what you've always gotten." Those are words of wisdom not only for those going through divorce, but also for those who face retirement. Monday mornings are good times to think in new ways.

Here are three ways we might begin this process:

First, we might practice giving ourselves permission to be different; allowing ourselves to do things when we feel like it, not simply because it is expected. So much of our working life is spent conforming to other people's schedules. We are unaccustomed to the freedom to do what we feel like doing. The very act of leaving a lecture before it is over, or putting down a boring book when it is only half-finished, is an act of "permission giving." This is unique for many, especially for those of us who grew up with our parents saying: "Finish what you've started," or "It's Saturday and you will clean your room."

Second, begin to build a new internal clock. This calls for us to be aware that the clock we are constructing is uniquely our own. From infancy, when we were fed on a schedule, and throughout our working lives, most of us have been on someone else's time schedule. Even if we exercise a degree of freedom in our choices, unconsciously we will use a criteria that is not uniquely our own. As we build our own internal clock, which enables us to make choices, we no longer have to wonder whether it is expected. We can now begin to ask: "Is what we plan to do satisfying for our souls?"

And, finally, make a radical shift in your understanding of this new stage in life. Treat everything you do as a part of a sacred pilgrimage, a journey that is filled with meaning. If we are able to re-image our lives in this way, we will find ourselves seeing our experiences in new ways and not using our normal conditioned responses.

Among persons in the interview process for this book was Frank, who shared with his wife the grief of having a son die in a riding accident about the time of his early retirement. Frank's company offered him the "golden parachute," which meant he could retire before age 62 or 65 with a sense of security. The couple sold their home and began splitting up their things and restructuring their lives.

"If you retire and stay in the home where you've been a long time, you probably would find yourself putzing around home," he said, "whereas in all our moves, we more or less buried some of our emotions in the business of our transitions."

Frank confessed to a sense of urgency to do things he said he wanted to do all his life. "My parents died when they were younger then my wife and me now. Losing our son made us more conscious of how much time we have to do these things. I think it all has made us become more accepting of what life offers."

We need to shift our understanding of life, understand the value of every day, and believe that we live in a world filled with a sense of the sacred. In a world of the sacred, the fingerprints of God are found all about us. Each moment is an opportunity to penetrate into the realm of the holy. Every incident allows us to connect with our soul.

It is Monday morning and the question remains: "Is this a pilgrimage or is it just the same old world?" The way we answer the question will determine whether we get out of bed or not.

The Healing of Memories

It is a dry white season
Dark leaves don't last, their brief lives dry out
And with broken heart, they die down gently
Headed for the earth
Not even bleeding
It is a dry white season, brother
Only the trees know the pain, as they stand erect
Dry like steel, their branches dry like wire.
Indeed, it is a dry white season
But seasons come to pass.

—Mongane Wally Serote[1]

"I did my part all those years on the job. Now that I'm retiring, I need something. Somehow I've got to learn to deal with all the garbage I've collected."

That is the cry for help of many retirees.

No one makes it into retirement without accumulating lots of garbage. And it is this garbage that leaves wounds on our souls; wounds in the guise of disappointments, letdowns, failures, and betrayals; wounds in the memories; relationships so hurtful that we have practically forgotten how they came to be.

There is much in our past we need to address. The pilgrim season is an opportunity to take care of that unfinished business. The pilgrim season is a time we can start to heal the memories from past stages of life.

"We are our scars." It has been said by many. Each of us carries wounds from long-gone encounters. For some, they have become scar tissue. For others, they are still open wounds. As I write these words, I can almost feel the rough edges of the wounds collected through the years.

Let the past be past, we often say. It is not pleasant to dredge up the garbage of former days. Why bring up the unpleasant wounds? But, deep down inside, we know that it is only by reflection on the "not so good" that we can walk confidently into the future.

Much as we would like to dismiss what was hurtful from earlier times, it seems to stick with us. The hope in the pilgrim season is that we can lessen the pain of those long, restless nights. Time alone does not heal. Time and distance can give perspective, but time itself cannot be mistaken for healing. What hurt us 20 years ago still lurks in our memories.

One of the early interviews for this book was with Elizabeth, who lives in a retirement community. She came to the interview in her golf clothes, having just come off the course. Elizabeth and her husband retired in their mid-to-late 50s. He owned his own business, and she was director of nursing at a hospital.

"We decided to sell my husband's business, but we weren't sure what we were going to do," she explained. "In fact, my husband came home one day and said that somebody had come to the office and offered to buy his business. He had planned way ahead financially and was tired of running it, so the sale went through.

"My husband thought I'd keep working, because I really enjoy nursing. But I said: 'If you're going to play, I'm going to play too.'"

While they hadn't planned what they would do in retirement, they did decide to try living in another part of the country. Then, she continued, the unexpected happened.

"We suddenly were involved in a terrible lawsuit, having to do with a store we owned in the Northeast. We were sued and in the litigation, with all of the appeals, rejections, and lies, this was the worst of times. My husband was such an honest man, and he had worked so hard all of his life. Then along came this slimy person and bilked us out of a lot of our retirement. We went to trial, and although the jury sided with us, the judge turned around the verdict and awarded the decision to this awful character."

Clearly, Elizabeth has had to wrestle with all of this garbage of the past in her retirement years.

"If I think about it, it's a bad memory. I can go

for weeks without thinking about it, but it was really hard on my husband. In fact, I blame that incident for his early death. I know if he were alive today, he'd still be mad about it."

When asked how she had replenished her life, Elizabeth replied: "I think I'm very fortunate. I have a strong Christian faith. My kids grew up healthy and intelligent, and my grandchildren are great. When I look around, sometimes I wonder how I've been so fortunate. I also do some work at the clinic that we started at the church, and I do some medical things, which I enjoy, and I play lots of golf."

All in all, Elizabeth is making a good recovery from the garbage that invaded her life. She ended the interview with, "I only wish I could put the trial and that awful man out of my mind." The scar from the wound is still there, but Elizabeth has taken the first step to recovery, admitting the presence of the wound.

Through the years, we've become such artful dodgers that we've learned to cover over any trace of these wounds. "Out of sight, out of mind" has been our philosophy. But difficult as it may be, the way to begin is to locate the scars. Review the garbage, if not with a trusted friend, at least by yourself. Start by asking, "Where in my life have I felt wounded?"

The tendency is to make long lists of all the garbage, the resentments, the hurts, and the angers that you have accumulated. Inevitably as you do this, you will begin to focus on certain people. This phase of the exercise quickly reduces itself into a blaming operation. Even when it seems impossible to locate someone to blame other than ourselves, surprisingly we can always find some person to whom we can point the finger of guilt. If you are really desperate in this game, there is always God.

The problem with this phase of the exercise is that if you stop here, you will end up feeling like a victim. As long as you can transfer the blame to other people, you can avoid any feeling of responsibility. Many of us have become experts at transferring guilt to others. We are professional prosecutors. We are adept at laying guilt trips on others. A friend has a T-shirt that says: "When it comes to guilt trips, I'm a frequent flyer." But being a frequent flyer can be self-defeating.

Frederick (Fritz) S. Perls, co-founder of Gestalt psychology, understood the difficulty of sinking into a blaming attitude and being trapped in the guise of a victim.[2] After articulating resentments, he frequently led his patients into an exercise of listing what it was that they could appreciate in their situation. For Dr. Perls, this process was the key to healing the memory of past wounds. It doesn't negate the hurts and disappointments; it simply places them in a different context. If we can accomplish both steps faithfully, we can heal many of the wounds of the past. Our wounds will no longer be a disease that permanently stamps our lives. Instead, they will be viewed as experiences that can be put behind us as we enter into the pilgrim season.

To heal a memory is not to blot it out, erase it, or even change it. Selective amnesia, which seems so easy, rarely works in reality. To heal a memory is to neutralize a history, to alter a malignant memory into a benign one.

Some contemporary spiritual writers have taken this process and placed it in a religious setting. They recommend going through the same steps as Perls, but taking it a step further. The final step is to locate God in the wounding circumstance. This is often easier said than done. I can recall reflecting on wounding situations and being unable to find God. Many people trying this process are unable to find God. They come to a conclusion that is neither orthodox nor terribly satisfying. They become what I call "closet dualists." They believe that good things come from God and wounds come from the devil (or whomever they associate with the author of evil).

The more sophisticated can maintain the façade of not being a closet dualist by holding the position there is something redeemable in even the worst of garbage. This may be true, but it is difficult to support in the face of great hurts.

One final approach, which grows from a number of writers who have wrestled with wounds, is to suggest that the past not be fixed. The garbage in our past is not to be seen as standing in immobile vaults, piled high in immovable mounds. Instead they would argue, the past is subject to rebinding or retelling. It is possible, they contend, to reinterpret what has happened to you. What seemed significant and what powerfully shaped your life 10 years ago would now appear trivial and unable to influence you.

The real secret to healing memories is to emphasize the future. If we were to believe that we are defined not primarily by our past, but by our future, many of our wounds would not have power over us. Seasons come and go and garbage happens, but the past is not as crucial to those who have found the secret. The healing of memories is one of the great challenges found in the pilgrim years. As some have said, the experiences we have had are not what define us; it is what we do with what has happened that counts in the long run. Some see retirement years as the end of a long struggle. A pilgrim focuses on the journey ahead.

CHAPTER SEVENTEEN

Death as the Framework

Begin. Keep on beginning. Nibble on everything.
Take a hike. Teach yourself to whistle. Lie.
The older you get the more they'll
Want your stories. Make them up. Talk to stones.
Short out electric fences.
Swim with the sea turtles into the moon.
Learn how to die.

—Ellen Kort[1]

It is so easy to appear an expert. You let it be known you have a doctorate, some sort of a title, and a following, and people expect you know all about your subject. In this chapter, I find myself uncomfortable. For obvious reasons, writing about death is not the easiest of subjects. But somehow, in the stage of retirement, death is a significant ingredient in our understanding.

A retired person of my acquaintance was overheard saying, "I seem to be spending most of my time either at funerals or writing letters of condolence." The older we become, the more likely it will be that friends and family will be dying. Each funeral we attend is a reminder of our own mortality. Barbara Fried's words could be the bottom line for retired persons. She wrote: "Death is the frame for the picture of this stage in life."[2]

Recently I attended a workshop on aging. The leader asked us to write down how many years we thought we had to live. It was a difficult exercise, not only because of the unknown length of life, but also because we were asked to plan our remaining years. In the course of the workshop, participants often had become aware of the shortness of their time on this earth.

Years ago, a book was published titled, *How Could I Not Be Among You*.[3] Ted Rosenthal, the author, was told he was dying of cancer. When he realized it was not a bad dream, he began to write down some of his thoughts.

"I don't think people are afraid of death," he wrote, "What they are afraid of is the incompleteness of their lives. I think what society does is strip you of your self-confidence from the moment you are born…strip you of the sense that what you are, is all you're ever going to be. And it isn't until you have discovered that you are going to die that you realize that whatever it is that you have, you've already got right there. And it doesn't matter if you die then or a million years from now."

Retirement for some is the time that we come to terms with the fact of our own death. When this happens, we see the end of ambition, the end of all we have been so earnestly striving for—power,

126

status, success, you name it. It's also the beginning of an awareness that what we have is all that we need. When death becomes the framework for life, we begin to realize that whatever we were searching for in life is already present.

The image of a person riding an ox while looking for an ox describes so much of our lives. All at once you discover the ox you have been so earnestly searching for is what you have been riding all along. The task in the pilgrim season is not to create something brand new. It is to become aware of what already exists within you, to recognize and appreciate what is already here.

*Un*awareness is the problem. Some of us keep searching, even in retirement, but certain events remind us of the shortness of our time. And when this happens we can have a breakthrough. A breakthrough into awareness, where we can say "yes" to what we are and "yes" to what we have become. Thomas Merton, the Roman Catholic priest, called this awareness "the breakthrough to the already."[4] The awareness of our mortality is often triggered by this breakthrough.

Most of us do not have the luxury of choosing the method, or the time of our dying. But that does not deter us from thinking about death and what it all means. Sometimes we are given a glimpse, a portent of the end. It may be through a near fatal heart attack, or it may come when attending a funeral and you come to the realization that someday you will occupy a similar coffin or be the subject of a similar memorial homily. Whatever the event, from that moment on, your life will never be the same.

There are some who recognize that the clock is ticking and our days are numbered. But for those who go deeper and have one of those breakthroughs to the already, they need no longer fear the inevitability of death. Ancient wisdom tells us: If you can begin to see death as an invisible, but friendly, companion on your life's journey, gently reminding you not to wait till tomorrow to do what you mean to do—then you can learn to live your life rather than simply passing through it.

Let us be honest: Anticipating death makes even the best of us uncomfortable. As a small child when we said our nightly prayers and came to the line, "If I should die before I wake," there was a feeling of unease. We are not at ease with the sense that death could be close. It is one thing to think of death as a friend, it is another to anticipate its being just around the corner. For some, this energizes us, for others, it makes us feel anxious.

Harvard psychiatrist Robert Coles made a study of what the near presence of death does to people. One of the interviews he recorded was of a factory worker for whom the world changed by coming into the presence of death.

Here are his words: "Twice, just twice, have I stopped and asked myself, 'Who are you, Mister, and what are you doing here? And what would you be doing besides what you have been told by your boss and your neighbors and everyone else?' It was after my father died. It was when my little boy fell sick and had leukemia, they thought. And for a month we stared death in the face with him. And for a month I wasn't the same person I usually am. They decided he didn't have leukemia and he'd be all right. And I told my wife that I had never lived like that before. All the wondering about the world, all the questions I asked. I don't mean my questions were so good, and I know everyone asks questions sometimes. But I asked them with my whole heart."[5]

Raising questions with the whole heart, living in the now with all that we have and all that we are, having a breakthrough to the already—these are the tasks of the pilgrim season when death is the frame for the picture.

The other day, I awoke, thinking as usual about all the things I had to do. As I got up and began to brush my teeth, I looked in the mirror and had one of those moments of discernment. In the pilgrim season we are given another stab at life, another chance to get it right. But I also understood, as I looked at the aging wrinkles, I might not have too many opportunities left.

CHAPTER EIGHTEEN

To Those in the Helping Professions

Earth's crammed with heaven
And every common bush afire with God
But only he who sees takes off his shoes
The rest sit around it and pluck blackberries.

—Elizabeth Barrett Browning[1]

There is an amusing joke told about the Communist Party in the United States. In the late 1940s, the party was suffering from a bad reputation and was at the same time desperate for members. The leaders came up with a unique idea to increase membership. They announced, during the year, that a $50 reward would be given to any member who recruited one new member. For two new members, the member would be given $50 and permission to leave the party. And a member who recruited three members would collect $50 and a certificate declaring that he or she had never been a member of the party in the first place.

Fifty years ago, I joined the church. At the time, the person who instructed me in the faith said, "To be a member of the church, you have to accept a calling as a minister." Not being the type to be half-hearted, I chose to become a professional minister, a priest, who was a recruiter as well as a life-long caregiver.

After 40 years in that role, it seems strange to no longer have a job. Does retirement mean that you have permission to cease being a priest? Or does one's calling continue? This is the dilemma for those in the helping professions. In retirement, we need the reassurance that the commitment we made so long ago does not cease when we leave our particular place of work.

There is a wonderful *Peanuts*[2] comic strip that I have kept through the years. In it, Snoopy sits in the first frame with his face silhouetted against the bright, full moon. He is wide-eyed and can't sleep, so he trots over to Charlie Brown's front door and kicks on it. Bam, bam, bam. Meanwhile, Charlie Brown himself is sitting up in bed unable to sleep. In the next frame, Charlie is at the front door and saying to Snoopy: "Are you upset, little friend? Have you been lying awake worrying? Well, don't worry. I'm here." Then you see him hugging Snoopy, consoling his friend and declaring: "The flood-waters will recede. The sun will shine tomorrow. And I will always be here to take care of you." Then we see Snoopy walking away from the encounter looking more peaceful. Charlie Brown yells at him one last time: "Be reassured." The final frame shows Charlie Brown back under the covers, staring into space, unable to sleep, mumbling: "Who reassures the reassurer?"

This is a particularly urgent issue when the reassurer retires. Who ministers to the minister, who heals the healer, who counsels the counselor? This is even more acute when in the past the helper has not been able to disassociate himself from his role. Is a doctor always a doctor? Is a priest always a priest? For most of us the answer would be "yes and no."

Yes, because we do not cut off our calling when we reach a certain age; no, because the community does not recognize the validity of one's calling past a certain age. Or at least there is an implied message: "Do not exercise your calling because this takes a job away from a younger person."

Several years ago in a workshop I was asked to list 10 words to describe who I am. Then I was told to rank them in order of importance. After completing this task, the leader instructed us to draw a line through the bottom seven words. He then asked how we would feel if we lost those bottom seven labels. Would we be any less of a person? If one of your bottom seven was your role as a helper, then retirement probably will not be very traumatic. But if your persona as a caregiver is one of the top three, the chances are that your transition will be difficult. This is particularly so if you have been in the limelight playing a significant role in the community.

Generally, there are three or four stages that a caregiver goes through when retiring. At first, there is a feeling of impotence. No longer are we looked upon as a reassurer. No longer do we have access to the many resources that we took for granted, such as secretaries, a pool of volunteers, and the support of grateful people.

Second, there is the feeling of isolation. Before retirement, we functioned with a staff, people who were dependent upon us, and a social life centered on those to whom we ministered.

And, third, there is a feeling of vulnerability. Those masks (Jung uses the word *personae*) we have spent a lifetime developing—the professional healer, the busy priest, the sought-after advisor—all now seem to be invalid. The professional helper begins to feel open to all sorts of pressures from which his former role protected him.

There is a fourth and final stage for some: the beginning of seeing ourselves in a different light. This involves us in reassessing the meaning of the roles or refashioning the masks we have worn through the years.

On a recent flight to Miami, I was engrossed in a book and not listening to the flight attendant as she went through the safety routine prior to take off. All of a sudden her words penetrated my subconscious. "In case of emergency, your mask will appear." Was this some kind of universal reassurance? Did this mean that our masks as helpers or caregivers would appear when needed?

The problem with this message is that we are to form new masks in the pilgrim season. The community no longer legitimizes the old roles. Our status is changed. Our power base is gone, and people relate to us in new ways. In the twinkling of an eye, one finds oneself as a sheep instead of a shepherd, the one who is ministered to, rather than the minister, being healed in place of being the healer.

The secret to making this transition is not to disregard your calling, not to throw away the old masks. The key is learning to become an amateur. In our society, the word amateur has suffered bad press. In common usage it seems to designate someone who isn't trained, of limited competence, and, at best, one who pursues a task with little skill and on a part-time basis. But, if we could recapture the older usage of the word we would be able to see how retirement does not stop our essential callings. The English word amateur comes from the Latin root, *amare*, which is the verb *love*. In its original intent, an amateur was a person who did whatever she or he did for the sheer love of it. An amateur was not paid to do something. He or she did it for the sheer pleasure. Recapturing the sense of being an amateur, in the old usage, is an important step in retirement for the caregiver in the pilgrim years.

Because the amateur does whatever he or she

does for the commitment to the game, rather than for an external reward, the amateur need not be limited by the context. Someone who loves football need not have a stadium and all the latest equipment in order to play the game. So it is with the retired caregiver.

When I met Mary, a professional nurse who, toward the end of her career, had been in teaching, research, and nursing administration, she had been retired for three years. She explained that she retired at 62 because she was at a point where she would have to get much more involved or get out and make way for other professors of nursing.

At first she traveled extensively, took golf lessons, attended movies, and in general spent many hours in leisure. "After a while I needed to feel that I was contributing and not just having fun," she said.

She reasoned that she had a lot invested in her education: "I put myself through school, and it seemed ridiculous to just stop and throw it all away." Then she said a "heaven-sent opportunity came along." The minister of her church invited her to be the parish nurse.

"I remember the first time my minister approached me. He said something like, 'I'd like for you to be part of my team.' And I thought: Oh no. I want to retire. Then I reflected on it, and, well, I prayed about it—and then I thought it really is an opportunity. We have a great number of older people in our congregation, and I enjoy working with older people. Some are not well, and I thought maybe I could help. I don't mean that I do anything magical. I am simply trying to help people connect and to know that others care.

"An example of what I do is if someone is hospitalized, I try to be there and help interpret what's going on. I see myself bridging that terribly complex hospital world with what's going on in someone's life," she explained.

Mary said she feels a power outside of herself prodded her to take on this new role. "I feel extremely needed, and yet I'm a volunteer. This puts me in a different role, and I don't relate in the same way with the medical profession. I think people [in the church] see me in a different way. Before this I used to sit very quietly in a back pew. Now I get to meet a lot of people. I don't feel like a different person...I feel just like I'm more allowed to be me.

"One thing I've learned since retirement," she continued, "is that happiness comes from wanting what you have and not wanting what you don't have. I've been much more satisfied with my life since retirement. Before, I was always seeking something else. Now I just enjoy what I have."

Fortunately, one doesn't have to be a nurse, doctor, minister, or other professional caregiver to gain satisfaction in life by filling the needs of others. All moments are times of healing and of ministry. A simple shared cup of coffee or a time of greeting a friend can be the context of healing and of ministry. Each moment is a part of eternity. And one's calling goes way beyond ordination, or licensing, or degrees. The amateur constantly walks on holy ground, where we no longer need sit around waiting for professionals to show us the way.

In the pilgrim season, the caregiver can truly begin to see him or herself in a new light.

CHAPTER NINETEEN

How Often
We Run Out of Time

What happens to a dream deferred?
Does it dry up
Like a raisin in the sun?
Or fester like a sore
And then run?
Does it stink like rotten meat?
Or crust and sugar over
Like a syrupy sweet?
Maybe it just sags
Like a heavy load,
Or does it explode?

—Langston Hughes[1]

When I first decided to enter the ministry, I recall sitting down with my mother. She was extremely disappointed to hear of my decision. She had always imagined that her only son would follow in his father's footsteps and work on Wall Street.

"Mother," I said, "I know this is not what you had hoped for, but I have decided to go to seminary and become an Episcopal priest." There was a long silence in which she looked to see if I was in my right mind.

Finally, in almost a whisper, she replied: "How long will it take you to become a bishop?"

Our dreams and the dreams of our parents are not always fulfilled by the time we retire. Sometimes when we reach the age of retirement our dreams are left hanging in the air like those good intentions that never really were completed.

We've all been there, the time of life when we come to the realization that many of our dreams will never happen. A number of expectations, hopes, fond wishes of parents, will remain on the books, but will never be fulfilled. As Spanish writer Miguel Unamuno[2] said: "It all comes down to one thing. We've run out of time." When we retire we run out of time; we cannot accomplish all the things our parents hoped for us. But more importantly, we cannot finish all the dreams we had for ourselves.

No one reaches retirement without feeling some sense of disappointment. We all have dreams that have been deferred, lost, postponed beyond where we could recover them. We all have been carefully taught that our goals ought to be completed. This understanding begins in childhood, when we are given stars on our papers if we finish our assignments. Then we are told that we are good boys or girls if we accomplish what had been expected.

As we get older, we receive trophies or diplomas in recognition of fulfilling a goal. Then, when we are still older, it is the large bank account, or the office with the expansive window that tells us we have lived up to our dreams or to someone's expectations. For many of us, there are some dreams that are never completed. We tend to carry not only a feeling of disappointment, but also a feeling of guilt. It's a thin line between the statements, "I'm disappointed in not fulfilling a dream," and "I am a disappointment and a failure for not accomplishing certain expectations."

But these feelings need not be. The pilgrim season is a time when we can reflect and learn from our disappointments rather than mourn our failures. Here is a stage in life in which we can take stock of our dreams and begin to see that not all dreams were possible, nor were they particularly right for us. Some goals are not worth pursuing. Perhaps we have failed to take into account what our gifts and talents really are. Perhaps we've never taken the trouble to prioritize our dreams.

You have heard it said that no one on his deathbed wishes he had worked harder. As a priest I have been with many people during their last moments. What I have observed is that people often regret the dreams they have pursued and wish they had revised their priorities. The pilgrim season is a time when we can do this.

We can drop those dreams of former days and take on a new set of goals more consistent with who we are and where we want to end our lives. The one message we must hear in the pilgrim season is that we have the capacity for beginning again. Elie Wiesel, the Nobel Prize winning author, very succinctly summarized it: "When He created man, God gave him a secret. And that secret was not how to begin, but how to begin again."[3]

This thought was expressed by one of the retirees interviewed for this book: "I have found that retirement is trying out new things and beginning again those things that I had formerly done. For example, I've gone back to one of my early loves, the piano. The other day I went down to a recording studio, played for two hours and made a CD of all my favorite tunes. I had never done that before. I did it for my family. It was a product that, hopefully, they will enjoy long after I'm gone.

"I'm just having fun beginning again some of my old passions that didn't have anything to do with making money or getting ahead in my work."

The secret in the pilgrim season that enables us to begin again is learning to substitute a few words for those that we usually use when speaking about former dreams. More often than not, when we reflect on those unfulfilled dreams, we use words like "if only." If only I could have done more or tried harder or been luckier. The secret is substituting the words "in the next stage" for "if only." When we are able to do this, it automatically changes our perspective from grieving over the past to emphasizing the future. This prepares us for beginning again with new dreams and a different vision of who we are and where we are going.

In the pilgrim season we are asked to see ourselves in an entirely different way and see the world through new lenses. The task is to see yourself as a person of value who counts, because you have emerged into this new stage. In this stage we are being invited to be a co-creator with God in re-imaging the world. In this stage we are called upon to be an explorer of our inner world of choice. There is a sense of excitement because we can view our very existence with new eyes. In retirement, we can say I am what I am, and I need not be apologetic. I need only to accept myself and rekindle a new set of dreams.

What an exciting prospect for someone who never did become a bishop.

CHAPTER TWENTY

Seeing Ourselves
in a New Light

Have you not known? Have you not heard?...
He gives power to the faint, and strengthens the
powerless. Even youths will faint and be weary,
and the young will fall exhausted; but those who
wait for the LORD shall renew their strength,
they shall mount up with wings like eagles, they
shall run and not be weary, they shall walk and
not faint.[1]

—Isaiah 40:28-31

My understanding about retirement did not come
all at once. It was a slow, painful sense of experi-
mentation and reflection. It started with clearing
out my desk and then spread to getting rid of much
of the baggage accumulated through the years. It
involved many starts and stops, many faltering
steps and petty failures. Somewhere in the first year
I came to the realization I was free to make many
choices—and the only real failure was not to choose.
I could choose to continue the worn-out scripts of

my past, backing and filling to make up for the losses experienced through retirement. Or, I could take some risks, throw away old scripts and begin to fashion a new me out of the bits and pieces I chose to keep.

One of the more troublesome things I discovered through this process is that we live our lives like actors in a movie. We are handed a certain script early in life, mostly shaped by our parents' expectations, the social milieu to which we were born, and our educational opportunities or lack thereof. Then, we simply act out our parts until we become no longer fit or are burned-out from the role.

From time to time, as we mature, we are given some insight into these scripts. Usually these moments of awareness come as we transition from one stage of life to another. It is at these moments that we can choose to either reject parts of the script or continue on until circumstances or our physical limitations dictate that we lay aside the script and begin searching for something new.

One of the final interviews for this book was with Brad, a retired professional dancer and professor of dance at a state university.

"The time finally arrived," he said. "After 40 years of teaching, I've finally discovered time to find out about my basic identity. I've worked hard all my life at getting credentials and arriving at a career. I find that now in retirement most of that falls away. Not that I don't value my accomplishments, but in retirement I'm really enjoying finding out about my basic personality.

"In spite of appearances," he continued, "I'm really very introverted. But with a career in the performing arts and teaching and lecturing, most people see me as extroverted. Frankly, I learned how to make that pay off. But it always took a toll, and I think I didn't realize the cost through the years. Being upfront, visible, audible, and all the responsibilities that go with that, created a lot of tension. Not unhappiness, I enjoyed my career, but I've gradually begun to realize that I need more introverted time. I've had to go back to be who I am as a basic person, not as the practiced, credentialed, wage-earning, college professor.

"Since retirement, hours in a day will go by, and I haven't been bored half an instant. There is a kind of continuous joy. From time-to-time I have to find some new little projects, but they usually appear. Or, I take a break and read, which is a real pleasure. Or sometimes I just sit and think about life. I'm finding that I'm a very reflective person."

It was early afternoon and a pleasant day when I visited Brad, and he met me in his garden. He explained that while saying goodbye to his working life, he had used his professional and artistic skills to create his new interest, his "strolling garden," which can be defined as a place where the flowerbeds and paths are active, yet meditation is encouraged as you walk along the way.

"I've discovered that working in a strolling garden involves a lot of heavy-duty work," Brad explained. "There are plank bridges, which I painted, and a stone wall with boulders that I rolled and struggled to pick up and carry.

"This particular garden is more like choreography than one might think," he said. "What it's relating to is a very basic instinct about the movement of things in space and time, and I've always been fascinated with that. For example, one thing I liked best about dancing was the lifting. You need a good sense for where the center of gravity is in a partner. The particular challenge was how to lift and carry women around a stage, sensing space and time and volume and weight. So this project of a strolling garden has used many of my skills. It has been a real joy."

In pondering the attitude of Brad and others interviewed, it appears that the basic questions are: Can you change the way you see life? Can you change the way you measure success? Can you change the very way you look at yourself and relate to others?

I do not think it comes about simply by waking up one morning and declaring: "I am now a pilgrim!" Nor does it happen by packing one's bags and pretending that suddenly you are ready to take a trip.

I suspect it begins to happen when we put more trust in the future and less reliance on the past. I suspect it happens when we take more risks and search for new challenges. I suspect it happens when we begin to walk with God, rather than walking alone with a sense of rugged individualism. There's a wonderful inscription above a university library: "The generation that knows only itself is destined to remain forever adolescent."

The goal in retirement is neither longevity nor acceptance. The goal is maturity, and that can only happen if you become a new you, a person willing to live the questions, to re-image yourself as a pilgrim and make the effort to search for meaning. As Rainer Maria Rilke has said: "Be patient toward all that is unsolved in your heart...try to love the questions themselves like locked rooms and like books that are written in a very foreign tongue... Perhaps you will then gradually, without noticing it, live along some distant day into the answers."[2]

If someone who knew you a long time ago were to bump into you and start a conversation, would they say when finished: "I sensed something different. There's something there. I can't identify it, but there is a difference. There's a different look in the eyes. There seems to be an air of excitement about life. It's as if he (or she) were a pilgrim, ready to move into new challenges, not surrounded by problems, but ready to move into new opportunities."

In view of the change Brad expressed in his interview, I asked if others had noticed a change in him since retirement?

"Well, a few old associates of mine detected

a change," he said. "One of them came up to me recently and said, 'What's the matter with you? Are you sick?' 'No,' I replied, 'I'm just discovering I'm not quite the person I've been.' She was incensed and said, 'I don't know how to react to you anymore.'"

Brad's youngest son, Bill, also detected a considerable change. "He and I go to lunch every once in a while," Brad explained, "and he reported to my wife, 'Boy, Dad is different now.' Well, I wasn't particularly aware of that. It might be in part the fact that I listen to him more, but I think it's also because I speak more reflectively. I refer back to my own personal experiences that are in various ways parallel to his when I was his age."

As I write these words, I am aware of several ways I've failed in my own first faltering steps in retirement. I am at times inconsistent, and no one knows better than those closest to me how much I can talk a good game and not act it. Yet, I still can dare to believe that somehow I can begin to see myself in a new light, that I can imagine myself to be a pilgrim, that I can learn to live with the unfinished, that I can walk in faith with a God who has given me the strength, if not to fly, at least to walk on an exciting pilgrimage, even though at times I may be weary.

Lots of people want their religion to make them feel secure as they enter into retirement. But security is not the goal, and religion is not simply a means to a happier life. Religion is only the courage and hope to face the unfamiliar and be able to move with hope into an inner journey of discovery.

The last word is to see yourself as a pilgrim on a sacred journey as you face retirement. Always remember, as Lao-tse said 2,500 years ago, the longest journey begins with a single step. I invite you to take that first step as you walk together with God.

Sources

Preface
1. Dag Hamaarskjöld, *Markings*, (New York: Alfred A. Knopf, 1964).
2. Carl Jung, *The Stages of Life, Collected Works*, (Princeton, NJ; Princeton University, 1969).

Chapter One: The Great Adventure
1. Dag Hamaarskjöld, *Markings*, (New York: Alfred A. Knopf, 1964).
2. Robertson Davies, *The Manticore*, (New York: The Viking Press, 1972).
3. Harry Chapin, *A Legacy in Song*, Cherry Lane Music Co., June 1987; Warner Bros. Publishing, March 2001).

Chapter Two: Choosing the Right Time
1. W.H. Auden, *For the Time Being*, (London: Faber & Faber, 1943).

Chapter Three: Finding a New Path
1. Dietrich Bonhoeffer, *Letters and Papers From Prison*, (New York: MacMillan Co., 1971).
2. C.S. Lewis, *Mere Christianity*, (San Francisco: Harper, 2001).

Chapter Four: The Way of the Pilgrim
1. William Bridges, *The Way of Transitions*, (Perseus Publishing, 2001, pg. 84).
2. T.S. Eliot, *Four Quartets* (London: Faber & Faber, 1968).

Chapter Five: Say it Isn't So
1. Nanao Sakaki, *Break the Mirror*, translation by Gary Snyder, Copyright 1996 by Nanao Sakaki. Reprinted in *Traveling Mercies*, by Anne Lamott by permission of Gary Snyder. *Traveling Mercies* copyright 1999 by Anne Lamott, published in the United States by Pantheon Books, a division of Random House, Inc., New York, and simultaneously in Canada by Random House of Canada, Ltd. Toronto.
2. Roger Gould, *Transformations: Growth and Change in Adult Life*, (New York: Simon and Schuster, 1978).

Chapter Six: Expecting the Worst
1. The Gnostic Gospel of Thomas
2. Karl Menninger, American psychiatrist, who, with his father and brother, founded the Menninger Clinic in Topeka, Kansas. In 2003, the clinic moved to Houston, TX.
3. Marcus Aurelius, *Meditations*, (London: Everyman #9, 1937).
4. Dion Fortune, in the preface of *Psychic Self-Defense*, (Samuel Weiser reissue paperback, 1992).
5. New Testament, John 10:10.

Chapter Seven: I'm Too Young for This
1. Dylan Thomas, *Do Not Go Gentle Into That Good Night*, *Collected Poems*, (New York: New Directions Publishing Corp., 1952).
2. *On Golden Pond*, (TCI, a Mark Rydell film, written by Ernest Thompson, produced by Bruce Gilbert, directed by Mark Rydell, 1981).
3. George R. Bach and Peter Wyden, *The Intimate Enemy*, (New York: William Morrow & Co., 1969).
4. The Book of Common Prayer, (1979, page 429).

Chapter Eight: The Business of Busyness
1. "Serenity Prayer." Commonly attributed to Reinhold Niebuhr. Adapted by the founders of Alcoholics Anonymous 12 Step Program.

2.   Thomas Kelly, *Testament of Devotion*, (New York: Harper & Row, 1941).

3.   Anne Lamott, *Traveling Mercies*, (New York: Pantheon Books, a division of Random House, Inc., 1999).

Chapter Nine: How Quickly We Are Forgotten

1.   T.S. Eliot, "Little Gidding," *Four Quartets*, (London: Faber & Faber, 1968).

2.   Old Testament, Ecclesiastes, Chapter 2.

Chapter Ten: Well, Dear, What Are We Doing Today?

1.   Maya Angelou, from a speech made at Trinity Institute, Grace Cathedral, San Francisco, 1985.

Chapter Eleven: It's Nice to Know Where You're Going

1.   Frederick Buechner, *Godric*, (New York: Atheneum, 1980; San Francisco: Harper & Row, 1983).

Chapter Twelve: There is No Such Thing as Retirement

1.   Sam Keen, *To a Dancing God*, (New York: Harper & Row, 1970).

2.   Nadine Stair, *If I Had My Life to Live Over*, (Watsonville, CA: Paper-Mache Press, 1992).

Chapter Thirteen: Withdraw From the World?

1.   Caroline Lejeune, British film critic, *The Quotable Woman*, compiled and edited by Elaine Partnow, (Los Angeles: Corwin Books).

2.   Old Testament, Genesis 4:10.

3.   New Testament, Matthew 25:35-40.

4.   Alice Walker, *The Color Purple*, (New York: Washington Square Press, 1982-83).

5.   Erik Erikson, *Childhood and Society*, (New York: W.W. Norton, 1950).

6.   New Testament, Luke 15:11-32.

Chapter Fourteen: Saying Hello and Goodbye
1.   W.H. Auden, *For the Time Being*, (London: Faber & Faber, 1943).
2.   Alanon: an organization that helps families and friends of alcoholics recover from the effects of living with the problem drinking of a relative or friend.

Chapter Fifteen: It's Monday Morning
1.   Maya Angelou, "On the Pulse of the Morning," delivered January 20, 1992 at the inauguration of William J. Clinton as President of the United States.
2.   *Garfield,* comic strip by Jim Davis.

Chapter Sixteen: The Healing of Memories
1.   Mongane Wally Serote, "The Night Keeps Winking," (Gaberone, Botswana).
2.   Frederick S. Perls, *Gestalt Therapy Verbatim*, compiled and edited by John O. Stevens, (Moab, Utah: Real People Press, 1969).

Chapter Seventeen: Death as the Framework
1.   Ellen Kort, *If I Had My Life to Live Over*, (Watsonville, CA: Paper-Mache Press, 1992).
2.   Barbara Fried, *The Middle Age Crisis*, (New York: Harper & Row, 1976).
3.   Ted Rosenthal, *How Could I Not Be Among You*, (New York: Avon, 1975).
4.   Thomas Merton, *Raids on the Unspeakable*, (New York: New Directions, 1972).
5.   Robert Coles, *The Call of Stories*, (Boston: Houghton Mifflin Co., 1989).

Chapter Eighteen: To Those in the Helping Professions
1.   Elizabeth Barrett Browning, "Sonnets From the Portuguese," Book 7.
2.   *Peanuts,* syndicated comic strip by Charles Schultz.

Chapter Nineteen: How Often We Run Out of Time

1. Langston Hughes, *Norton Anthology of Poetry*, (New York: W.W. Norton & Co., 1983).

2. Miguel de Unamuno, Spanish philosopher, essayist and poet, 1864-1936, "Poesias."

3. Elie Wiesel, *Messengers of God*, (New York: Random House, 1976).

Chapter Twenty: Seeing Ourselves in a New Light

1. Old Testament, Isaiah 40:28-31.

2. Rainer Maria Rilke, *Letters to a Young Poet*, translated by Reginold Snell (London: Sidgwick & Jackson, 1945).